Enchantment of the World

MALAYSIA

by David K. Wright

Consultant for Malaysia: Dr. Charles Reafsnyder, Indiana University, Bloomington, Indiana

Consultant for Reading: Robert L. Hillerich, Ph.D., Bowling Green State University, Bowling Green, Ohio

CHILDRENS PRESS ®

CHICAGO

Village homes set on stilts in Pinang

Library of Congress Cataloging-in-Publication Data

Wright, David K.
  Malaysia / by David K. Wright.
      p.   cm. — (Enchantment of the world)
  Includes index.
  Summary: An introduction to this small independent
tropical country.
  ISBN 0-516-02702-6
  1. Malaysia—Juvenile
literature. [1. Malaysia.] I. Title. II. Series.
DS592.W725 1988   87-33784
959.5—dc19   CIP
                                                AC

Picture Acknowledgments
© **Cameramann International Ltd.:** 4, 9 (right), 12
(2 photos), 13 (left), 58 (left), 60 (2 photos), 62 (top), 72, 73
(left), 74, 75, 76 (right), 78 (right), 85 (left), 87 (left), 93
(2 photos), 95 (top & bottom right), 101, 103
(3 photos), 104 (bottom left), 107, 108 (top & bottom left),
110 (right), 111, 112, 114 (2 photos), 115 (3 photos)
Shostal Associates: cover, 5, 11, 91 (right); © J. David Day:
cover (inset),14, 16, 21 (right), 22, 23 (left), 31, 50 (bottom),
53, 59, 64, 66 (left), 76 (bottom), 108
(bottom
right); © Manley Photo-Tuscon, Ariz.: 25, 97 (left); © E.
Streihman: 56; © Vic Maratea: 95 (bottom left); © Herbert
Lanks: 110 (left)

©**Photri:** 6 (top), 26, 32 (right), 54 (bottom), 65 (left), 67,
70, 82, 87 (right), 88, 97 (right), 99 (2 photos)
© **The Photo Source/Three Lions:** 6 (bottom)
Journalism Services: © Al Guiteras: 9 (left), 21 (left), 57
(left), 65 (right), 104 (bottom right)
Root Resources: © Tom Hanley of Bloomsbury: 13 (right);
© Yoram Kahana: 18 (right), 100; © Kitty Kohout: 19
(right); © Ruth Welty: 54 (top); © Mary A. Root: 66 (right);
© Byron Crader: 78 (left); © Rita Ariyoshi: 79; © Jane P.
Downton: 106 (top & bottom left)
H. Armstrong Roberts: 19 (left), 20 (right); © H. Thonig:
17, 18 (left)
Valan Photos: © Robert C. Simpson: 20 (left); © Y.R.
Tymstra: 23 (right); © Christine Osborne: 80 (top), 84, 91
(left)
Historical Pictures Service, Chicago: 28, 32 (left), 34, 36
(2 photos), 37, 39
AP/Wide World Photos, Inc.: 43, 44 (2 photos), 45, 47, 49,
69
Tom Stack & Associates: © George D. Dodge & Dale R.
Thompson: 50 (top)
Third Coast Stock Source: © Ted H. Funk: 57 (right), 58
(right), 62 (bottom left & right), 85 (right), 104 (top), 106
(bottom right)
© **Norma Morrison:** 73 (right)
Len W. Meents: Maps on 8, 94, 98, 102, 105
**Courtesy Flag Research Center, Winchester,
Massachusetts 01890:** Flag on back cover
**Cover: Petaling Street, Kuala Lumpur; Mt. Kinabalu,
Sabah (inset)**

A member of the Bajau, Muslims who originally came to Malaysia from the Philippines

TABLE OF CONTENTS

Above: The shoreline near the city of Kuantan on the east coast
Below: Rice fields in Sabah

Chapter 1

WELCOME TO MALAYSIA

Malaysia has no welcoming Statue of Liberty. But for hundreds of years, immigrants have sought safety and freedom in this tropical land in Southeast Asia. Newcomers have arrived because the country is along an ancient trade and migration route between India and China. The first inhabitants—called *orang asli* or original men—still exist in the northern hills of the mainland peninsula. Tribes almost as primitive live in the two states on the island of Borneo that are a part of the country. No one knows how long any of these primitive people have lived there. They are a minority dwelling in jungles that might frighten a modern Malaysian.

Two regions make up the nation of Malaysia. Peninsular (formerly West) Malaysia is on the mainland of Southeast Asia just below its northern neighbor, Thailand. Just south of Peninsular Malaysia is Singapore, and across the Strait of Malacca is Sumatra. Sarawak and Sabah (formerly East Malaysia), on the northern part of the island of Borneo, about 400 miles (644 kilometers) across the South China Sea from the peninsula, is the second region. Within Sarawak is the small nation of Brunei, which is politically separate from Malaysia.

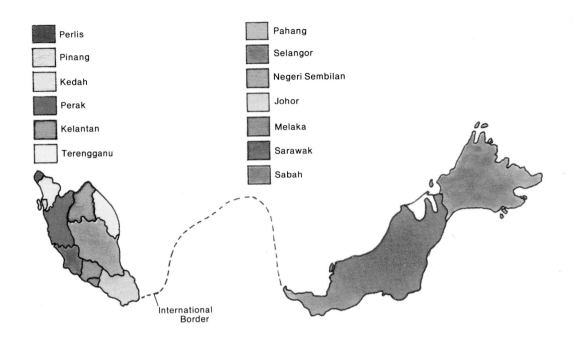

MALAYSIAN STATES

In some ways, Malaysia has changed little since time began. The country includes eleven states on the mainland peninsula; Johor, Kedah, Kelantan, Pahang, Perak, Selangor, Terengganu, Negeri Sembilan, Melaka, Pinang, and Perlis, and the two states on the island of Borneo; Sarawak and Sabah. Malaysia has miles of unspoiled beaches and is just 60 miles (97 kilometers) north of the equator. It is 127,317 square miles (329,749 square kilometers) in size, slightly larger than the state of Arizona or the country of Poland.

TOPOGRAPHY

Peninsular Malaysia is a land of jungles—flat to the west, with mountains in the middle, and numerous rivers and bays to the east. The two offshore states, Sarawak and Sabah, have jungle-covered foothills and mountains. The highest peak between Asia's great Himalayas and New Guinea is in Sabah.

Some modern industries in Malaysia are automobile manufacturing (above) and oil refining (left).

MODERN MALAYSIA

The land is unchanging, but the people are changing dramatically at this very moment. Once considered a backward country of little importance, modern Malaysia has a constitution and free elections. It is a capitalist system and is among the world's most productive nations for its size. Timber, cars, clothing, and more come from mills and factories and from labor done in the home.

Agriculture and mining also are important. Rubber, palm and various fruit trees, rice paddies, and gardens help support the country's more than nineteen million inhabitants, with two or three crops a year possible. Beneath the earth lies tin, which is mined throughout the peninsula. Except for oil, resources of the two island states have yet to be fully explored. The land is not fertile everywhere, yet real economic progress has taken place. In fact, the country is one of the most prosperous in all of Asia, along with Japan, Singapore, and Brunei.

THE PEOPLE

Three distinct people live in Malaysia. The Malays usually dwell in rural areas, frequently farm, speak Malay, and practice the religion of Islam. They make up more than 50 percent of the population. Persons of Chinese descent, most often found in the country's larger cities, represent about 35 percent of the population and are Buddhists, Taoists, or Christians. Indians, usually of the Hindu faith, make up about 10 percent of all citizens. Usually they are either city dwellers or live on rubber plantations.

To complicate matters, many Chinese and Indian Malaysians speak one or more of a dozen languages and may not know a word of Malay. At present, many Malaysians—no matter who their ancestors were—know enough English to communicate with each other.

English is spoken on the streets of major cities and even by a few residents of small villages, because Malaysia was, until 1957, under British control. Due in part to the British, Malaysia enjoys good public health, highways and railroads, and respected school systems.

Malays are the dominant political force in the country. Like Malaysian Indians and Chinese, Malays tend to vote as a unified group in elections and are therefore able to control the government because they are in the majority. As a result, they were able to establish their religion, Islam, as the country's official religion. At the same time, however, the country's constitution guarantees freedom of religion to all groups. The Malay control of government through the ballot box also means that the majority of civil service and government related jobs are filled by Malays.

A Malay family

Malays guard their political control carefully because the minority Chinese have traditionally controlled the country's economy. By the time Malaysia achieved its independence from the British in 1957, the immigrant Chinese had a near total monopoly on Malaysian owned businesses in the country. Because many of these businesses were family owned or part of the activities of Chinese clan associations, non-Chinese were excluded from many types of employment in private enterprise no matter how well qualified they might be. These barriers, added to the agricultural background of Malays, resulted in a major division of wealth in the country with Chinese having an average household income twice that of Malays.

To protect themselves from the economically dominant Chinese, the politically dominant Malays enacted certain rights as the founding population of the country. Later, in 1971, Malay, Indian, and Chinese political parties jointly enacted additional

Left: An Indian mother and child
Right: A Chinese family enjoying a meal in an outdoor restaurant

"affirmative action" laws designed to alleviate Malay poverty through better educational and employment opportunities. These laws were encompassed in a plan called the "New Economic Policy."

A major goal of this policy was to achieve, by 1990, a 30 percent Malay ownership of the commercial and industrial activity in the country with Malaysian Indians and Chinese controlling 40 percent. In 1969, Malays owned only 2 percent of the business in the country. In education, the New Economic Policy established programs for Malays designed to enhance scientific, technical, and vocational skills. These programs sent many thousands of them to universities in Great Britain, Australia, and the United States. Since 1971, Malays have made significant progress, but are still well short of the goals set for 1990.

Left: A sign in Bahasa Malaysia, English, Chinese, Arabic, and Indian
Right: These women represent the three principal groups in Malaysia: Indian, Chinese, and Malay.

Conflicts between Malays and Chinese over these and other matters have resulted in violence between the two groups, but, in general, Malaysians have been able to resolve their differences through peaceful means. In spite of their disagreements, both groups respect one another.

The government has successfully increased tourism by promoting the people's religious, artistic, and cultural differences. Primitive people who were headhunters only one hundred years ago now entertain cruise ship passengers. Malaysia probably has more festivals each year than any country on earth. And maps and signs point the way in several languages to Hindu temples, Buddhist shrines, and Moslem mosques.

As long as the country continues to prosper, Malaysia will be a pleasant place to live.

*Evidence has been found to prove that men lived
in these caves in Sarawak forty thousand years ago.*

Chapter 2

TWO LANDS, ONE COUNTRY

Bird's nest *soup?*

That's just one of the unusual items from the lands that make up Malaysia. The nests are built by millions of swallows in caves on the island states of Sarawak and Sabah. Malaysians climb spindly pole ladders up the sides of these huge, tree-high caverns to retrieve the nests for cooks all over Asia who prepare Chinese food. There are caves on the peninsula, too. Like the island caves, they were formed by water working through limestone.

THE LAND

Water has played an important part in the development of the country. Several large rivers, fed by rainfall, are navigable for more than 100 miles (161 kilometers) upstream from the coast. For millions of years, these wide, slow-moving, muddy rivers have washed away many soil nutrients and minerals. Scientists know that this action has taken place without change, because Malaysia is one of the few countries on earth with no hurricanes, tornadoes, earthquakes, or active volcanoes.

The Rajung River in Sarawak

Except for an occasional flood—which speeds the washing away—the land has existed without a major catastrophe. What is left? Rocks, of course, and a reddish, claylike soil. This soil is less than perfect for growing plants. But because rainfall each year is from 65 to 200 inches (165 to 508 centimeters), amazing varieties of plants and animals are found.

Rain forests cover two-thirds of all the land. These forests contain twenty-five thousand kinds of trees and fifty-five thousand kinds of flowering plants, shrubs, herbs, and vines. The tall trees are so thick that little sunlight can reach forest floors and there is not a lot of undergrowth. Instead, in the rainy season, muddy soil is everywhere. In the dry season, the forests can be easily walked without special equipment or precautions.

Elsewhere, along some of the coasts, there are swamps. These swamps are thick knots of mangrove trees that grow on muddy tidal flats. Birds and animals make their homes in such places.

A mangrove swamp

There are many different kinds of birds and animals in other places, too. They especially like land that has been cleared by man, then abandoned. This scrubby grassland and second-growth forest makes up about 7 percent of the total land area.

PLANTS

If all the plants bloomed at the same time, the rich aromas would be overwhelming. However, different kinds of plants bloom at different times throughout the year.

Trees blossom, too. They bear fruit and lose leaves in different months. The rain forest provides a very important crop throughout the year: hardwood lumber. Beautiful ebony, teak, and sandalwood, hardened by years in the warm, damp climate, are made into smooth, sturdy furniture. In contrast, the reedy bamboo tree is used for almost everything, from food to scaffolding. It

Many fruits are grown in Malaysia, including bananas (left) and durians (right).

grows wild, and is planted in thick clusters around Malaysian homes for a bit of privacy. Each segment of bamboo holds water. Jungle visitors who know this, tap the bamboo trees when thirsty.

Other trees commonly planted near homes are coconut palm, guava, papaya, the reliable banana tree, and one of Asia's favorites, the durian. This tree produces round fruit each June that, when broken open, smells like rotten garlic. But Malaysians hold their noses and dig out the middle, which has a custard texture and a wonderful taste. The durian is so smelly—and so popular—that hotels throughout the country have signs warning, ''No durian eating allowed!''

The rafflesia is the world's largest flower. It grows in the Borneo jungle and has a blossom a yard (.9 meters) wide. It is a parasite and grows on stems and roots of other plants. It, too, has a bad odor.

Varieties of pitcher plants also lack a sweet smell, but are of great interest. These small plants lure insects, usually ants, into

Orchids (left) and a hibiscus (right)

their cups. Then the sticky substance that draws the ants begins to consume them. The panicky insects cannot climb up the walls of the pitcher because they are covered with a waxy substance. Tiny thorns around the edge of the cup also keep the ants inside. Soon, the plant's digestive juices overcome the small intruders. Scientists have found this juice capable of digesting egg whites or raw meat. For a plant no bigger than a bar of soap, that's quite a feat.

Smelling much sweeter and very pleasant to see are some of the country's other flowers. One symbol of the country is the orchid, which grows wild and in gardens everywhere. A popular vacation souvenir from Malaysia is an orchid coated in pewter, which is 97 percent pure tin, mined in the country. Still other flowers, such as the hibiscus, are so fragrant that it's easy to see why perfume was invented in the Far East.

An elephant (left) and an orangutan (above)

ANIMALS

Malaysia also has a variety of animals. Elephants still run wild in the interior of peninsular Malaysia. The rare, two-horned rhinoceros exists in remote parts of Sarawak and Sabah. Other large animals include the seladang, a huge wild ox, plus tigers, civet cats, bears, deer, wild pigs, tapirs, anteaters, crocodiles, and lizards. Almost as big are dozens of different kinds of monkeys, including the rare orangutan (which means "man of the forest").

No animal has a more colorful past than the elephant. Traveling in packs, the huge, gray animals have been known to raid gardens, destroy small villages, and circle back on hunters who were stalking them. One large beast even charged and derailed a train many years ago. Weighing 6,000 to 8,000 pounds (2,722 to 3,629 kilograms), they are smaller and lighter than African elephants. They can be tamed and trained to haul logs and perform other tasks during their life span, which may stretch to

Marboks (left), singing jungle birds, and butterflies (right) mounted for sale

seventy-five years. Sadly, some people still hunt elephants, killing them for their beautiful ivory tusks.

At the other end of the scale is Malaysia's most delicate resident, the butterfly. More than nine hundred kinds of butterflies, some with wingspans larger than this page, flutter all over the country. They are even exported, traveling home with tourists mounted in attractive frame boxes, their red, blue, green, or yellow wings unlike any moth or butterfly anywhere else.

As attractive as the butterflies are the birds. They come in all shapes, sizes, and colors and include several kinds of eagles amid hundreds of colorful, tropical varieties. The island states have many more rare birds than the mainland, in part because Sarawak and Sabah are 90 percent forest. The birds and cave-dwelling bats dine on millions of disease-carrying mosquitoes and other insects, as they help spread plant pollen.

Not all jungle dwellers are so nice. Rats thrive in the rain forest, in villages, and in major cities. Visitors to farm areas tell of being

The Temple of Azure Cloud, more commonly called the Snake Temple, is filled with poisonous pit vipers. The snakes are objects of worship because they are thought to be related to the mythical dragons of Chinese folklore.

kept awake at night by the sound of rats chewing through heavy wood into the rice supply. Wherever it's damp and leafy, there you will find leeches. No larger than a thumbtack, they are thin as leaves. The sightless creatures crawl or drop from trees onto humans and animals, sucking blood until they swell to an inch or more thick. They then fall to the ground, leaving a small puncture mark and an irritating itch.

Other ground residents include cockroaches, black or brown and sometimes as big as a fist, all of the usual ants and beetles, and the scorpion. Scorpions look like crayfish but have a high, arched tail containing a poisonous stinger. A scorpion sting is always painful and sometimes fatal. So are bites from some of the country's 170 kinds of snakes.

Most snakes are harmless, but fifty different kinds are poisonous. Many of those live well out into the Indian Ocean or the South China Sea. Six different land snakes are extremely dangerous: two kinds of cobras, two kraits, and two coral snakes. Of these, the king cobra is the largest poisonous snake on earth. It can reach a length of 18 feet (5.5 meters). But that is small compared to the giant of the jungle—the python.

Left: Sun drying ikan bilis   *Above: A leatherback turtle*

The powerful python can reach a length of thirty feet (nine meters). It disposes of animals by squeezing the breath out of them and then swallowing them whole. Many farm animals, some as large as pigs, are eaten each year by pythons. As the country becomes more developed, pythons retreat farther into the rain forest. Most residents know of them only from visits to the zoo.

ANIMALS FROM THE SEA

In contrast, Malaysians go no farther than the local market for a look at the sea's inhabitants. Many of the most popular dishes feature fish, prawns (large shrimp), squid, octopus, and other sea dwellers. An especially well-liked snack is *ikan bilis*, handfuls of dried fish no bigger than birthday candles. These silvery creatures are sold in every market and are dried everywhere—including areas of seldom-traveled blacktop road.

The country's most famous seafarers are the leatherback turtles. Large enough to be ridden, these slow-moving monsters wade ashore each June on the east coast of the peninsula. They nuzzle into the sand, lay soft-shelled eggs, and then waddle back to the sea. Leatherbacks have been sighted as far away as the Atlantic Ocean, yet Malaysia is the only place where they lay their eggs. So, for the newborn turtles, swims of thousands of miles await them.

There are other animals, from soft-shelled turtles to deer, *pelandok*, which are no larger than cats. All find a home in a land where a central spine of mountains is covered with dense forests.

NATURAL RESOURCES

Rainwater, churned into streams and rivers, creates inexpensive electric power for the country, though streams are not developed in Sarawak or Sabah.

Beneath the surface of the peninsula lie rich deposits of tin and iron ore. The east coast shows promise in oil exploration, as do the states on the island of Borneo. Other minerals of varying importance include bauxite (used to make aluminum), copper, mercury, gold, and coal.

Open-pit tin mining and the cultivation of rubber trees are two of the oldest jobs on the peninsula. In very similar ways, both were made possible by weather. The Chinese came to Malaysia in sailboats blown along by the northeast monsoon. They were experienced miners and were soon digging tin out of the ground with great enthusiasm. Residents of India, equally experienced on rubber plantations, sailed to Malaysia on the southwest monsoon and saw the demand for rubber grow as the world auto industry began. The Chinese and the Indians liked what they saw and decided to stay. Among the things they liked was the weather.

Tapping trees on a rubber plantation

CLIMATE

The climate is tropical. It is influenced by the annual monsoons (great winds) that move back and forth across the Indian Ocean and south Asia. The land is drenched during two different, but very warm, periods in May and June and in October and November by daily showers. Then, the rains stop. Each monsoon is followed by a time of clear, hot weather.

There are four seasons in Malaysia, but seasonal differences are slight. Year round the sun shines, even during monsoon seasons, before and after the rain, creating steamy days of 90 degrees Fahrenheit (32.2 degrees Celsius). Rain is less predictable during the other months, though knots of clouds are usually somewhere in the sky. It is always cooler and wetter in the mountains.

A small settlement on the east coast of the mainland

Chapter 3

FAR EAST CROSSROADS

A MEETING OF DIFFERENT PEOPLE

From the beginning, many different kinds of people called Malaysia home. Because nearby lands offered better hunting or farming, Malaysia was settled by an overflow of people. Chinese from the north, Indonesians from the south, islanders from the east, Indians from the west—they edged into the country from all directions.

What did these very different settlers find? They discovered a rugged land thinly populated with shy and primitive people. The native people retreated farther into the jungle and the hills. They chose not to meet and learn from the newcomers. So the newcomers met and learned from each other.

The reason for this very early meeting of different people is easy to see on a map. Malaysia is Southeast Asia's major intersection. Sailors, traders, hunters, and farmers either came and went or came and stayed. But whether they stayed or left, they were exposed to different ways of living. This resulted in a culture that was neither Chinese, Indonesian, island, nor Indian, but a mixture.

An early illustration of a village in North Borneo

Speaking of mixtures, "Malaysia" is a term invented from the term "Malaya." Malaya was the traditional name for the peninsula. But the name was modified in 1957 when Sarawak and Sabah became part of the country, even though they were 400 miles (644 kilometers) away on the island of Borneo.

FIRST SETTLERS

The first migrants may have come from southern China about 4000 B.C., traveling down the peninsula and spreading to the islands in the South China Sea. That wave was followed by explorers from India before 2500 B.C. The ancestors of today's Malays came north from the islands in the South China Sea two thousand years later. Since then, many other people have arrived: various South Pacific islanders, Thais, Burmese, Arabs, Portuguese, Dutch, English, and Vietnamese. Each has added to the country's character, charm, and vitality.

PIRATES AND INDIANS

Indians on their way to China created the first great civilization. They sailed along Malaysia's west coast, stopping about two thousand years ago to build ports. Here they decided whether to carry their goods across Malaysia or brave the ocean voyage around the southern tip of the peninsula, where pirates ruled.

The pirates were Indonesian and other South Pacific people, while the merchants on the east coast and on the island of Borneo were Indian or Chinese sailors. Indian settlements were established throughout Southeast Asia, leaving Hindu and Buddhist influences in today's arts and languages. At different times, kingdoms founded by Indians to Cambodia, Java, and Sumatra ruled all of the Malay Peninsula and nearby islands.

PARAMESWARA

The smartest ruler of all may have been Parameswara, who lived on the island that is now Singapore. He and his people were chased off the island by invaders, so they traveled north along Malaysia's west coast before finding a pleasant site near the mouth of a river. They began the city of Malacca there in A.D. 1403.

Parameswara was tired of being worried or chased by pirates, so he made a deal with a Chinese emperor. In exchange for China's protection, Parameswara gave the emperor gifts and his loyalty. This agreement attracted many ships filled with cargo to trade and scared off enemies.

Malacca's control continued to expand with the rulers who followed Parameswara, who died in 1424. The city spread its influence across the peninsula and controlled large portions of the nearby island of Sumatra. Malaccans were under one ruler, Tun Perak, who ruled from 1456 to 1498. Tun Perak built up a large army and spread modern laws throughout the region.

MUSLIM SAILORS

But it was Malacca's wonderful location that made it, by 1500, the busiest port in all Asia. Merchants from the East and West traded gold, gems, rare wood, spices, silk, and porcelain. They also stopped to take on food and water for longer voyages east or west. Chinese emperors may have guaranteed safety in the port, but sailors from northern India had a more lasting influence.

These Muslim sailors were deeply religious men who brought the faith of Islam from the Middle East. They spread the religion across the peninsula and into thousands of Indonesian islands in just a few years. Though Malaysians might trace their ancestry to half a dozen different races, they were under one god—Allah—by A.D. 1500.

In defense of their trading empire, Malaccans resisted attempts by Siamese and Burmese Buddhists to establish colonies or conduct raids. They subdued smaller states and ran Malacca so well that it attracted the attention of several European nations.

PORTUGUESE VISITORS AND THE SPICE TRADE

The Portuguese decided for several reasons to visit Malacca. First, they noticed that Venice, in Italy, was growing rich by trading with the Asian port. Second, the Portuguese had despised and feared Muslims since the Crusades a few hundred years earlier.

Santiago Gate is all that remains of the fort the Portuguese built in the sixteenth century.

Third, many Europeans believed there was an undiscovered Christian kingdom in Asia. And fourth, all Europeans wanted the spices found only in the Far East.

Why were spices in such demand? Because they were used to preserve food. Meat, fish, and other food that easily spoiled could be kept edible with pepper, nutmeg, cinnamon, cardamom, saffron, powdered chilies, and other ingredients. The exotic seeds and mixtures also brought flavor and variety to many dull, bland diets.

A Portuguese fleet landed at Malacca in 1509, seeking to set up a trading post. The strangers attracted the attention of Muslim traders, who rallied local residents and tried to capture the fleet. The boats escaped, but twenty Portuguese sailors were taken prisoner. This gave the Europeans a reason to return, which they did, in 1511.

The second Portuguese fleet was led by Alfonso de Albuquerque. Firing huge cannons, the invaders sailed up the Malacca River that ran through the middle of the city. They were able to knock down a bridge and level any building in their path.

Alfonso de Albuquerque (above), the Portuguese ruler who tried to monopolize Malacca's spice trade. Right: A contemporary spice market in Sabah

After weeks of fighting, involving the Malaccan ruler and many of his subjects, the Asians surrendered to the fleet of gunboats.

Albuquerque took control of the city. He built a fort with huge, thick walls and allowed only Portuguese to live within. This caused anti-Portuguese feelings, which may have been why Christianity failed to take hold among Malaccans. The Portuguese attended their own churches and either treated the local population badly or completely ignored them.

The new rulers tried to monopolize the spice trade. They did this by controlling the Strait of Malacca and charging tolls for all ships using the waterway. No wonder the Portuguese retreated to their fort on what seemed like an annual basis, fending off attacking warriors with heavy cannon fire behind the big walls of the fortress.

THE ARRIVAL OF THE DUTCH

Another wave of Europeans arrived in the late 1500s. These were the Dutch, and they had no more regard for the local population than did the Portuguese. The two European powers disagreed for several decades. Then, in 1640, the Dutch surrounded Malacca. They starved Malaccans and Portuguese into surrender in seven terrible months. But once the Dutch gained control of the city, the long war had made it unimportant. It was no longer a bustling port.

SUMATRAN AND OTHER SOUTHEAST ASIAN SETTLERS

The Dutch tried to revive Malacca, but ended up leaving only soldiers in the town to keep order. Fewer and fewer ships anchored in the old port and it became only a small Dutch outpost—one of dozens in Southeast Asia. Other parts of the peninsula attempted to attract trade, but no place was as successful as Malacca had been. Almost unnoticed, farmers from the nearby island of Sumatra began to settle in peninsular Malaysia in large numbers.

The Sumatrans were called *Minangkabau*, "buffalo horn," people because their buildings had rooflines that looked like the horns of a water buffalo. Land and authority were passed from mother to daughter instead of father to son. They also held free elections, even before such elections were held in the supposedly more advanced European countries.

Meanwhile, other Southeast Asians were trading aggressively with Europeans. Residents of the Celebes Islands, Java, and Sumatra gained money and power by selling spices, jewels, and more and by buying arms and various objects made of metal and glass. The peninsula was overrun by Bugis sea gypsies from the faraway Celebes Islands. They conquered, then accepted, the Sumatrans and Malayans.

Malay soldiers under Dutch rule

A TROUBLE-FREE TIME

The eighteenth century marks the last time for nearly two hundred years that the area now known as Malaysia could be considered free. Local sultans (rulers who were also Islamic religious leaders) conducted modest businesses in a number of small states. The Dutch and other traders kept most pirates on the run and potentially troublesome countries such as Siam and Burma were worried that they, too, would be subdued by Europeans.

Life for the average Malaysian was as enjoyable as anywhere else at the time. The weather was never violent; there was always enough water for crops; the fish almost seemed to swim into nets; and great varieties of trees and bushes yielded not only fruits and nuts, but fiber for clothing and material for houses.

On the other hand, the water was not always safe to drink; a scratch or an insect bite could lead to agonizing death from disease; and there was no warning to prepare villagers for invaders. Tigers, elephants, wild cattle, and snakes could and did kill people in seconds. Folk medicine seldom helped seriously hurt or diseased people. The pace of life may have been slow, but it was not easy.

Chapter 4

TECHNOLOGY ARRIVES

ARRIVAL OF THE ENGLISH

There is a legend about Britain's arrival in Malaysia that may or may not be true. In 1786, the first Englishman landed on Pinang, an island just off the west coast of mainland Malaysia. His name was Francis Light. He saw that the jungle was thick and that the natives he hired weren't eager to chop into it. So the adventurer loaded his ship's guns with silver coins and fired the money into the dense forest. The local employees frantically hacked their way toward the small fortune, thus clearing the land.

Soon, the British merchant fleet (then the world's largest) visited Pinang regularly. The island and its main city, George Town, became a port almost as busy as Malacca once had been. Chinese, Arabs, Indians, Siamese, Burmese, and Bugis all traded readily with the English, who wanted to make up for financial losses suffered in wars with the French and the United States in North America.

Before dying of malaria in 1794, Light was a tough and unforgiving boss on the island. He appointed local *kapitans* to oversee each ethnic group. These leaders were well paid to keep

James Brooke (left) and Sir Stamford Raffles (right)

their people in line and help the port run smoothly. But Pinang became less important as the British looked elsewhere for trade, and seamen anchored in ports closer to the Spice Islands.

THE FREE PORT OF SINGAPORE

The British assumed control of Malacca in 1824, but wanted another port between China and India. Sir Stamford Raffles and other British officials decided the perfect spot would be an unimportant island at the southern tip of the Malayan peninsula. The island, Singapore, was declared a free port (no taxes would be paid or collected on any goods passing through). Singapore quickly attracted all kinds of traders and sailors. It was such a success that by 1826 the British declared it, Malacca, and Pinang part of a special Straits Settlements trading area.

RULE ON BORNEO

On Borneo, a more unusual action was taking place. James Brooke, a British veteran of warfare in India, sailed a British ship

Brooke's ship, the IIMS Rinaldo, bombarding Salangor in the Strait of Malacca

to Sarawak in 1839. The world's third largest island was governed weakly and in constant rebellion. Brooke used his cannon to help a local ruler regain control. A year later, the ruler named Brooke *raja* (leader) of Sarawak. This was the beginning of more than one hundred years of peaceful, honest rule by the Brookes, some of whom were unusual. One of the Brooke rajas lost an eye as a child. He replaced it with a glass eye plucked from a stuffed bird in a taxidermy shop!

Controlling Sabah (then called North Borneo) was harder. Several generations of British governors tried to convince local residents that English ways were best. One rebellion, led by a heroic Saban named Mat Saleh, lasted from 1895 to 1905 and tied up hundreds of soldiers in this far-off corner of the British Empire. Fighting continued off and on until 1941.

GOODS BECOME READILY AVAILABLE

Europe was, in the 1800s, in the middle of the industrial revolution. No longer were most goods made in cottages and ships. Factories were making stoves, tools, machinery, clothing, shoes—anything for which there was demand. Items once owned only by kings could be owned by anyone for not much money. The raw materials for these goods came from such places as Southeast Asia. And no one traded with Asia more than the British.

In 1869, the Suez Canal opened. Ships from Europe no longer had to travel around Africa to reach Asia. Now they could sail into the Mediterranean and Red seas and then into the Indian Ocean. This saved weeks in rough waters and made European goods more available all over Asia. But it caused severe problems.

THE NEED FOR STRONG RULERS

More complex societies call for stronger, wiser rulers. The men who ruled nineteenth-century Malaysia were sultans. They knew Islamic law and their rich cultural heritage, and for many years, successfully operated tin mines. The British, with access to overseas markets, however, sought a rapid expansion of tin mining. Because the resident Malay population was already occupied in farming and fishing and not attracted to the harsh conditions of mines, they were not able to satisfy the very large demand for labor that accompanied British capital investment in tin, rubber, and public works. Hence, British colonial officials encouraged employers to bring in hundreds of thousands of Chinese and Indians who were either poor or landless in their own countries.

The Chinese migrated to Malaysia to escape their backward and overpopulated homeland. They worked hard and were pushed even harder by mine owners. To protect their few rights, the

Government House in Sarawak in the 1800s

miners organized secret societies. When injustice happened, a mine owner was warned. Failure to heed the warning meant a beating—or worse. Since many mine owners were Chinese, too, rival societies frequently fought large, noisy, and dangerous battles. Casualties were not limited to the Chinese. A British officer, J. W. W. Birch, was murdered as he bathed in a river in 1875. He had made the fatal mistake of assuming he knew what was best for both sides in an argument.

ENGLISH ADVISERS

Fortunately for everybody, there followed many fair-minded English advisers. Hugh Low in Perak and Frank Swettenham in Selangor, for example, realized they could look out for British interests and at the same time avoid interference in local affairs. They quickly gained the respect of everyone from the sultan to the local village chief. In many cases, the British adviser in a state turned to a multiracial counsel for guidance in ticklish matters. By 1914, all peninsular states, even the northern states obtained in the early 1900s from Siam (Thailand), had British advisers.

Kuala Lumpur became the capital of the Federated Malay States in 1896. Selangor, Perak, Negeri Sembilan, and Pahang made up the federation. Like many peninsular cities, Kuala Lumpur was founded at the point on a river where ships could go no farther. Wherever boats scraped bottom and were unloaded, there a town began. Other Malaysian cities founded in this way include Kuala Kangsar, Ipoh, and Alor Setar. The new capital was not much to look at. Its name meant "muddy confluence" and it was that. Surrounded by open-pit tin mines, K. L., as it is usually called, only had location in its favor.

DEVELOPMENT IN TRANSPORTATION AND INDUSTRY

Location became important, however, because the British built and maintained excellent railroads and highways. As better methods of growing rubber were employed, better ways to get it to market were constructed. English engineers constantly dredged all major ports. This prevented the many muddy rivers from choking off shipping.

The dredge, a method of continuous mining, also was used to meet the increasing demand for tin. Money to run the country came from taxes on all rubber and tin that was exported.

Rubber's success on the peninsula was a dream come true. Prior to 1870, only Brazil successfully grew these trees. When blights hit Brazilian trees, prices skyrocketed. The British planted the first rubber tree seedlings in Kuala Kangsar, between Kuala Lumpur and Pinang Island, and gradually a hardy plant developed. In the 1890s, coffee growers were persuaded to plant rubber, instead. When the automobile began to use rubber in quantity, many British and local plantation owners became wealthy. Many of the

British who started plantations in Malaysia had previously owned or worked on plantations in India. Because they were familiar with the work habits and temperament of Indians, these plantation owners preferred imported Indian laborers to Chinese or Malays. Consequently, thousands of workers from the south of India moved to Malaysia, where they worked on plantations with a high degree of skill.

A consistent British policy from the end of the nineteenth century until 1941 was to maximize the inward flow of people. Once in the country, authorities worked to induce the immigrants to remain. Female immigration from China was encouraged so that laborers would establish families and settle in, and official encouragement was given to the establishment of Chinese language schools. When Malays began, in the 1920s, to express well-founded fears that their culture and identity would be submerged by the influx of immigrants, the British responded that the Chinese were only sojourners who would return to China when their work was completed. But the British did not encourage Chinese to become assimilated to Malay life; indeed they emphasized the separateness of Chinese, Malays, and Indians. In the 1930s, Chinese Communists, supported from Red China, began to gain support among the Chinese communities in Malaysia.

ASIANS QUESTION EUROPEAN SUPERIORITY

At the beginning of the twentieth century, an event was taking place thousands of miles away that would affect all of Asia. In 1905 the Japanese defeated Russia in a war. This marked the first time that a "backward" country had beaten a world power.

People in Malaysia and elsewhere began to question the supposed superiority of the Dutch, French, English, and other countries with colonies. The British were able to postpone discontent in Malaysia by leaving each group largely to its own devices, and especially by leaving the ceremonial and religious affairs of the Malays to the Malay sultans and aristocracy. As the prosperity of the Malay states grew in the 1920s and 30s, the rulers became richer, enjoying more of the trappings of authority. The relationship between the British colonial administration and the Malay elite during this period was mutually beneficial.

On Borneo, development lagged. Fatal diseases, such as malaria and beriberi, were eliminated on the mainland but continued to kill hundreds of people in the Brooke family's Sarawak and in Sabah. A few strides were made, however. The Brookes convinced their many tribes that head-hunting was wrong and that warfare was the worst way to settle an argument. As World War II came closer, the island states remained overwhelmingly wild and often dangerous.

WORLD WAR II—THE JAPANESE INVADE MALAYSIA

A few hours after the Japanese attacked Pearl Harbor, in Hawaii, on December 7, 1941, they invaded the peninsula of Malaysia. Landing far to the north near Kota Baharu on the east coast, they headed south. Their goal was to capture the British naval base on Singapore island. Just ten weeks later, Japanese soldiers marched victoriously into Singapore with hundreds of British soldiers as their prisoners. They had captured all of Malaysia and now held the one base that would have prevented them from getting Indonesia's oil and Malaysia's rubber for

Australian troops fought the Japanese in the jungles of Malaysia during World War II.

warfare. Japanese losses totaled 15,000 men, compared to British, Australian, Indian, and Malay losses of 166,600.

Malays and Indians greeted the Japanese with open minds. But Malaysians of Chinese ancestry weren't so trusting. Japan had been fighting China since 1937 and immediately mistreated anyone they thought to be Chinese. Many Chinese went underground, forming guerrilla bands. They weren't always interested in politics, but some of their leaders were. Several leaders either already were or became members of the Malayan Communist party (MCP).

While a few Indians, seeking independence for India, aided the Germans at anchor in Pinang, Indians and Malays alike suffered under the Japanese. The conquerors had promised to return Asia to Asians, but instead the people were overworked, underfed, abused, and imprisoned. Late in the war, British soldiers parachuted into the jungles in small groups. They attempted to lead local forces, but spent most of their time trying to stay alive.

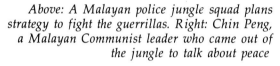
Above: A Malayan police jungle squad plans strategy to fight the guerrillas. Right: Chin Peng, a Malayan Communist leader who came out of the jungle to talk about peace

The tropical climate rotted uniforms and the rain prevented planes from dropping supplies. When jungle fighters did manage to harm Japanese, revenge on civilians was quick and terrible. So most Malaysians were jubilant when the Japanese surrendered in 1945.

GUERRILLA WARFARE CONTINUES

Japan's defeat failed to signal peace in Malaysia. Many guerrilla fighters who were Communists faded into the jungle. They attacked isolated outposts and plantations in well-armed bands. An emergency was declared in 1948, as British and local soldiers pursued the rebels. One method of beating the guerrillas was to deprive them of food or contact with rural residents. More than five hundred villages were moved from near the rain forest to more populated areas. When the Communists entered such areas, soldiers in ambush awaited them. Gradually, there were fewer and fewer rebels. Most moved back and forth across the Thai-Malay border. The state of emergency was lifted in 1960.

After Malaysia gained independence, Tunku Abdul Rahman became the head of the new nation.

FORMATION OF THE UNITED MALAY NATIONAL ORGANIZATION

Earlier, the British had decided to take power away from individual sultans. Malaysians on the peninsula protested, though financially troubled Sarawak and Sabah quickly agreed to become British colonies. In 1948, due to Dato Onn bin Jaafar, a leader in the movement toward independence, a federation was formed, instead. This put local control in the hands of the sultans, while forming a weak central government. The English made changes in Malaysian rule following the formation of the United Malay National Organization (called UMNO), founded by Onn bin Jaafar.

INDEPENDENCE

For the good of the country, and to prove that they were against the Communists, the Malay Chinese Association (MCA) joined UMNO. UMNO leader, Tunku Abdul Rahman, and MCA head,

Tan Cheng Lock, campaigned together in the country's first major national election in 1955. As a result, UMNO won fifty-one of the fifty-two seats. The British watched the new government take shape, then granted the country independence, or *merdeka*, on August 31, 1957. Crowds in soccer stadiums and on playing fields throughout the country cheered as the transfer of power ceremony was broadcast.

GOING IT ALONE

Tunku Abdul Rahman became Malaysia's chief minister in 1955 and was the person most responsible for leading the country to independence. Even before the British departed amid impressive ceremonies in 1957, Rahman was thinking for himself. He offered in 1955 to accept Communist guerrillas as citizens if they would lay down their arms, backing this offer with a dramatic meeting between himself and Communist leader Chin Peng in a remote area. But the meeting failed to produce an agreement, and Peng and his men returned to their jungle hideouts.

FORMATION OF MALAYSIA

The term "Malaysia" was not used until 1961, when Rahman, the son of a sultan who was trained as a lawyer, proposed that Malaya, Sarawak, Sabah, Singapore, and the tiny kingdom of Brunei join in an association of states under one flag. Rahman and other Malayans in these countries believed this display of unity would improve the economy and focus attention on Southeast Asia's Malayan-speaking people. But a larger country, that spoke the same language, stepped in.

Sukarno, president of Indonesia

The leader of nearby Indonesia, known by the single name of Sukarno, accused the states involved in the proposed association of plotting against his country. In 1963, he declared a badly planned war against Malaysia and the states included in Rahman's proposal. The Indonesians greatly outnumbered the Malaysians. But Malaysia had solid leaders and Indonesia had leaders who had been worked into a frenzy by Sukarno, a strange mystic. When poorly organized Indonesian soldiers landed on Malay soil, they were quickly killed or captured. Sukarno's dream of uniting all into Greater Indonesia ended in 1966 when he was overthrown.

Before he faded into history, Sukarno caused more problems for Malaysia. While getting his countrymen excited, he also caught the attention of Filipinos. They believed that they had a claim to Sabah, in part because Bajaus and other regional people living in Sabah were Muslims who originally came from the Philippines. But once the states joined in 1963, Filipino opposition declined.

Not all of the news was good for Rahman and his followers. Many Malays living in Malaysia were upset that Singapore was included in the association. The island state had a reputation as a Communist stronghold and was overwhelmingly populated by Chinese. The Malays (who called themselves *bumiputras,* or "sons of the soil," to distinguish them from Chinese or Indian Malaysians) did not want to join Singapore. So, as Brunei had done in 1963, Singapore backed away from the merger in 1965. That left Malaysia as we know it today—the mainland and two island states on Borneo.

RACIAL PROBLEMS

One of the reasons Rahman approved Singapore's departure was Malaysia's worsening racial situation. Several times since independence in 1957, conflicts have broken out between Malays and Chinese. Malaysians of Chinese descent sometimes stereotype Malays as lazy and ill-educated. The Chinese are stereotyped by some Malays as being money-hungry and godless. Both stereotypes hinder understanding between the two groups and neither does justice to the positive attributes and virtues of both peoples.

The departure of Singapore from the Malay Federation left Malays firmly in control as the dominant ethnic group in Malaysia. After more than a decade of independence, however, the distribution of wealth in Malaysia still overwhelmingly favored the Chinese. This led to increasing friction between the two groups and fears by Malays of being overrun by the economic power of the Malaysian Chinese. Following a hotly-contested election in May 1969, large-scale rioting erupted and several

*After the rioting of 1969, food packages were prepared
to hand out to the thousands of homeless people.*

hundred people were killed. The New Economic Policy was
implemented to correct the inequitable distribution of wealth
between the two groups and to counter the history of
discrimination against Malays by many Chinese employers.

MALAYSIA TODAY

Generally, the government has done a good job of running the
country since independence. Prime Minister Mahathir bin
Mohamad prefers to establish good business relations with other
governments. His reforms have included modernization in
manufacturing and technology, as well as better use of human
resources. Malaysia is now a major force in the world market.
Since independence, it has adopted what is useful from the
Western world while maintaining its own customs, culture, and
religion. Perhaps that should be the goal of any emerging nation.

Above: The modern building of the Department of the Interior in Sabah
Below: The Secretariat Building in Kuala Lumpur

Chapter 5

WHERE RELIGION RULES

Islam is important in both the activities of government and the daily lives of Malaysians. Malays, who are Muslims, decided before independence that Islam would be the official religion.

GOVERNMENT

Malaysia's government is loosely modeled on the British system; it is a parliamentary democracy with a constitutional monarchy. The constitution provides for a head of state and two elected houses of Parliament. The head of state is a king known in Malaysia as the *yang di-pertuan agong,* or "supreme ruler." He has largely ceremonial duties to perform. He and a deputy head of state are elected by the Conference of Rulers from among their number for a five-year term. The king is also the leader of the Islamic faith in Malaysia as are the sultans for their own states. The government is led by a prime minister who is appointed by the king, but is normally the leader of the party with the majority in Parliament.

Each state has its own legislature and constitution and controls land laws and laws of the Islamic faith.

According to the Malaysian constitution, the Supreme Court is the country's highest court. Below the Supreme Court, the High Court maintains appellate and revisional jurisdiction. Magistrates' courts and sessions courts compose the third level of the system. The lowest level is village courts for minor offences.

ISLAM, THE OFFICIAL RELIGION

To understand what role religion plays in the life of Malaysians, it is important to learn a bit about Islam. Islam began in Arabia in the seventh century. It came from the preaching and thought of the Prophet Muhammad. The religion teaches that Muhammad is the latest and most important in a line of prophets that included such familiar names as Abraham, Moses, Noah, and Jesus. Muhammad said believers must worship only God, whose name in the Arabic language is Allah, and that they must follow certain religious practices. The belief spread to India and from there to Malaysia.

THE FIVE PILLARS OF ISLAM

At first glance, Islam seems very simple. There are five pillars (rules) for becoming a Muslim. First, to become a member, a person must recite aloud what is called the profession of faith. "There is no god but Allah, and Muhammad is his Prophet." Second, a Muslim must pray five times a day, preferably in a house of worship, which is called a mosque. Third, a Muslim should pay a tax on land he or she owns. This money is primarily

The National Mosque in Kuala Lumpur was built in 1965.

for the poor. Fourth, Muslims must fast from sunrise to sunset during Ramadan, the ninth month of the Muslim lunar calendar. Fifth, every Muslim must make a pilgrimage once in his or her lifetime to Mecca, Saudi Arabia. This trip, called a *hajj*, involves a visit to a sacred mosque and praying while following a well-worn route all pilgrims travel.

There is much evidence of Islam's presence in modern Malaysia. Five times daily, the *muezzin* (priest) cries out in Arabic from every mosque in Malaysia, calling faithful Muslims to prayer. The call nowadays is over loudspeakers and echoes for blocks. Male

Above: The interior of the National Mosque in Kuala Lumpur, which has room for eight thousand people. Below: The Sabah State Mosque in Kota Kinabalu

and female Muslims use separate entrances into each house of worship. They remove their shoes, wash their hands, faces, and feet, and then stand facing a religious leader. He is elevated and chants prayers as members bow or lie flat on the floor. For each position there are specific prayers. Fridays are special days, with verses read from the Islamic holy book, the Koran. The prayer session at noon each Friday is considered the most holy and usually includes a sermon.

MOSQUES

Next to the call to prayer, the most striking thing about Islam in Malaysia is the dramatic mosque architecture. Middle Eastern designs have traveled across centuries and over half the world, yet they are virtually the same as mosques in Turkey, Egypt, or North Africa. Every mosque has a minaret, a tall, thin tower used originally to call the congregation to prayer. Since Islam prohibits art representing living things, intricate geometric designs are used for decoration. Many mosques have bulbous roofs that cover a large, open prayer room. This room in the largest mosques can hold twenty-five thousand worshipers or more. Marble tiles and numerous pillars make the interior of the mosque a cool and inviting place to pray.

ISLAMIC LAW

The faith affects Muslims and non-Muslims throughout the country. That is because Islam has a complex body of law that governs personal behavior. It calls for punishment that fits the crime committed. For example, in strict Islamic countries, people

The Leong San Tong Khoo Kongsi Temple in George Town, Pinang

convicted of stealing must lose the hand that stole. The law in Malaysia is a mixture of British and Islamic justice. Some laws apply to all persons, but others apply only to members of the Islamic faith. Drinking alcohol, for example, is forbidden only to Muslims.

BUDDHISM AND HINDUISM

Buddhism is the religion of the vast majority of Malaysians who trace their heritage to China. The Buddha or "enlightened one," was a prince named Siddhartha. He formed Buddhism in India eleven hundred years before the birth of Muhammad. The faith came to Malaysia from China, where it blended with Confucianism, Taoism, and ancestor worship. Buddhism teaches its followers that the ultimate goal is *nirvana* (salvation). The Buddha attained salvation by preaching the truth and making mankind realize what the truth is. Malaysian Chinese, like their

Left: A shrine hung at the entrance of a Chinese home. Right: The Reclining Buddha in the meditation hall at Wat Chayamangkalaram, Pinang, is 105 feet (32 meters) long.

ancestors, worship in ornate, red-and-yellow temples containing hundreds—even thousands—of Buddha images. If Islam has room for only one god, Buddhism believes there are thousands of Buddhas, or enlightened teachers.

Buddhism as practiced in Malaysia has been influenced by the ancient religions of mainland China. The Chinese worship their fathers, mothers, grandparents—any relative who died in the recent or distant past. Tiny altars with offerings of incense, fruit, or money are seen all over Malaysia, in the workshop and in the home. Malaysian Chinese have frequently emphasized the mystic aspects of religion, performing ceremonies that involve hypnotism or a worshiper entering a trance. Such ceremonies are easy to find. They are accompanied by drums and chants and feature huge, portable altars bedecked in fantastic colors. Any side street can be used for such performances, which last for up to thirty minutes.

The Hindu Sri Mahamariamman Temple was built in 1873. Left: Priests change the dress on the statue of Mahalakshimi, the god of wealth. Right: The exterior of the temple

Mysticism plays an important part in Hinduism, too. This ancient religion, with millions of gods in hundreds of forms, is practiced by Malaysians whose forefathers were Indian. Hinduism includes all forms of religion. The Hindu is taught to be tolerant of whatever kind of worship anyone chooses. That's due to the fact that Hinduism doesn't depend on the existence or nonexistence of a god. Instead, it is seen as a religion without a beginning or an end. It is all-inclusive, formless, involves endless rebirth, and allows individuals to emphasize whatever part of the faith they choose.

The symbols of Buddhism and Hinduism are as flashy as Islam's are sober and plain. Hindu temples contain dozens of idols — monkey gods, cow gods, human gods, devils, and more. Fragrant buds of flowers are hung on the various statues, making the altar rich and sweet. Both religions involve mystic ceremonies. Hindu priests, often wearing only a towel wrapped around their waists, spend vast amounts of time cleansing and decorating temple idols.

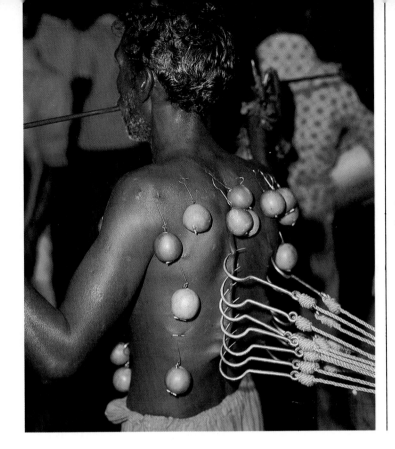

The Hindu festival of Thaipusam

A Hindu festival, *Thaipusam*, has men piercing their skins repeatedly and carrying heavy objects up hundreds of steps while in a trance. Also, many Hindus wear a dot of colored powder on their foreheads. The dot is a "third eye," a sign of added knowledge.

OTHER RELIGIONS

There are other religions in the land. Some persons whose parents or grandparents were Indian are followers of the Sikh religion. This religion blends Islamic and various Indian beliefs. A few Chinese practice Christianity, as do small communities of Portuguese and Armenians. Dozens of local religions thrive among the tribal people in the mountains and up the lazy, broad rivers on Borneo.

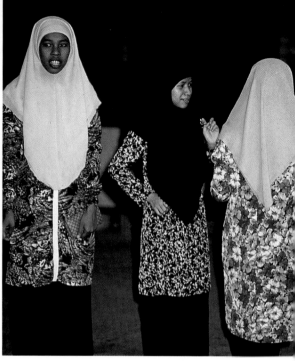

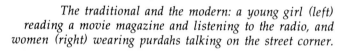

*The traditional and the modern: a young girl (left)
reading a movie magazine and listening to the radio, and
women (right) wearing purdahs talking on the street corner.*

MALAYSIAN TOLERANCE

The majority of Malaysia's Muslims realized from the start that
they would have to cooperate and coexist with Malaysians of
other religions and national origins. This makes Malaysia
somewhat unique in view of the recent rise of Islamic
fundamentalism throughout the Middle East and western Asia,
best seen in Iran. In Malaysia, the right of people of all religions to
practice their faith is protected in Malaysia's constitution.

For every sign of Islamic law in Malaysia, there is a sign of
Malaysian tolerance. Women in strict Islamic households never
leave their homes without wearing a *purdah*, a scarf that covers all
of the upper body except the face. In contrast, modern Malaysian
women in Kuala Lumpur wear cool, tropical dresses and work in
offices, both of which are prohibited in strict Muslim societies.

Muslim women—in Malaysia at least—may divorce and
remarry, own property in their own right, and inherit property
from their fathers. A number of Malay women also are prominent
in national offices.

Also, Muslims are warned constantly not to drink alcoholic beverages, yet beer is manufactured in Malaysia and is a common street-corner drink. Gambling is against religious law, but one of Malaysia's most popular resorts has an enormous casino. A recently formed political party, anxious to return the country to strict fundamentalism, was all but ignored during the 1987 national elections.

There are still more signs of Islam. A modern, high-rise building in Kuala Lumpur has only one job—to help pilgrims finance their trip to Mecca. Other big buildings in the capital are often banks, which presents an ethical problem for Muslims. According to their law, it is not right to seek interest on a loan or give interest for even the smallest savings account.

Elsewhere, "extremist groups" occasionally make the news. Several younger Muslims have been caught destroying Hindu idols. And at one of Malaysia's seven colleges, Muslim students recently warned female classmates to wear their purdahs at all times and not speak in class when certain subjects are studied. This last matter points to a crucial question for the country; can nation building take place in a Muslim society? Some Muslims don't believe that changes introduced from the West are always good. So there is some opposition to the many Malaysian students who attend colleges in England, Canada, the U.S.A., and Australia. But Malaysia's highly thought of public health system might not work as well as it does without students going abroad. And the students, when they return to their homeland, contribute a great deal and believe their country is a good place to live.

Hardly anyone, in fact, leaves Malaysia. The few who do are usually elderly Chinese who want to return to the mainland to visit relatives and live their final years.

Above: A new housing development in Pinang
Below: Bread (left) and housewares (right) for sale on the streets of Pinang

Chapter 6

THE ECONOMY

PRIVATE ENTERPRISE

Private enterprise has contributed to the material success of Malaysia. There are fifty newspapers in six languages, plus numerous radio and television stations. People tend to be well-informed, despite the fact that the government can censor news reporting. Large industrial ventures from overseas, such as a new auto assembly plant designed by Japanese in Kuala Lumpur, employ thousands. Because the population is growing, virtually every area has ambitious home construction under way. Like most Western nations, the number of homes under construction depends on the availability of loans. Malaysia has branches of banks from China, Hong Kong, Japan, Saudi Arabia, the United States, and elsewhere.

It seems that at least one member in every family is some sort of street vendor. Cool drinks, sweet snacks, blue jeans, T-shirts, books, religious articles, cassette tape recordings—these and other items are sold in the streets of large and small cities, night and day. In fact, many street vendors stay open until midnight or later, since Malaysians frequently wait until the sun goes down for their evening meal, often purchased outside the home.

A water buffalo is used to plow a rice field.

AGRICULTURE AND INDUSTRY

Rice is a major part of the Malaysian diet. The crop grows best in flooded or irrigated fields after being planted by hand. Earthen dikes separate one field from the next. Plowing is most often done in wet or dry fields with a water buffalo. Rice growers can nowadays produce as many as three crops a year. It is husked and either sold or stored, depending on the growers' needs.

Rubber trees, in perfect rows, are cut or tapped for their sticky, white sap. Workers collect *say*, called "latex," in bowls before noon each day. The sap flows best in the cooler part of the day. Acid is then used to turn the latex into thick slabs, which are rolled into sheets and dried in a smoking house. Smoking turns the latex dark brown. Malaysia is the largest producer of natural rubber in the world and rubber is one of its major exports.

Harvesting of tropical rain forest timber for furniture making

*Left: A man climbing a coconut palm tree Right: The oil from
oil palm seeds is used as a base for soap, margarine, and cosmetics.*

is important to Malaysia's developing economy. Protection of the
rain forests was a major topic at the 1992 Earth Summit held in
Rio de Janeiro. At this conference India and Malaysia argued that
forests are a national resource, not global, and that logging is
necessary to their economy.

The country is a leading supplier of palm oil found in processed
foods all over the world. All over peninsular Malaysia, food is
grown. Bananas are plentiful and always seem in season. They are
produced for local eating, since the smaller and tastier Malaysian
variety doesn't ship well. Pepper and nutmeg bushes, coconut and
cacao trees, plus numerous other foods are grown for export.
Sugar cane is harvested for home and foreign use.

Fruits come in an incredible variety, though few are exported.
Mangoes, grown in several varieties, have a smooth, yellow skin
and a large seed covered with sweet, orange flesh. They are juicy
and taste a bit like very sweet peaches. Mangosteens are round,

Starfruit (left) and papayas (right)

with hard purple-black skin. When opened with a sharp knife, sweet, juicy white segments are found inside. One must be careful when eating mangosteens, because the juice stains clothing. Papayas, almost as large as footballs, are originally from South America. Fresh pineapples are eaten on a stick or dipped in thick soy sauce and chilies. Pineapples are also canned. Rambutans are fuzzy, red fruit with juicy, white flesh. Starfruit have five sides. If they are cut horizontally, the piece of fruit will be star shaped. The starfruit is yellow and tart.

Malaysians enjoy a variety of fruit and gladly import whatever they don't grow themselves. Apples from the U.S.A., pears from China, grapes from Australia, and oranges from Africa are fruits sold in Malaysia—even in small villages.

FISHING

Outside villages near any coast, dozens of fishing boats called *prahus* are anchored. These brightly painted prahus bob out to sea

A fishing boat putting out to sea

each day in search of fish, one of the staples of the Malaysian diet. The catch includes carp, cockleshells, crab, cuttlefish, squid, and tiny ikan bilis. Even residents far inland enjoy fish, since much of the haul is netted and then dried or salted for later consumption. Fishing is best on the east coast, where the South China Sea is less polluted than the Indian Ocean on the west. Wealthy people from across the world come to the east coast to fish, where boats are still built by hand.

DRUGS

Opium, a product of a kind of poppy flower, is a narcotic drug. A thousand miles from Malaysia, in northern Thailand, eastern Burma, and northern Laos, the flower is grown by hill tribes. These people make thin cuts in the flowers, which allow a white juice to flow out. The juice dries and turns brown or black. Tribespeople sell this dried product in lumps, cakes, or bricks. In its legal form, the product can be made into morphine or codeine.

These prescribed drugs are painkillers, made for those who are ill or injured. In its illegal form, it is smoked or injected as opium, smoked or sniffed as heroin.

The drug was discovered in the Middle East almost two thousand years ago and was introduced in India in fairly recent times. The British brought opium to China in the 1700s and soon were making great sums of money from it. Pipe smoking, which began in America with tobacco, allowed the Chinese a quick way to consume opium. Millions eventually became addicted. Sadly, one of the reasons the Chinese were so easily addicted was that opium helps the user forget hunger. Only after China banned the substance in 1907 was the problem solved there. But wherever opium was banished, it became more expensive—and more desirable. Today, legal and illegal growing takes place mostly in Asia.

Used in Malaysia by Chinese miners to overcome hunger and pain, the drug was popular throughout the late nineteenth and twentieth centuries. Opium dens, where pipes were filled for customers, were as popular as pubs or taverns or beer halls are in other countries. The drug culture of the 1960s increased the popularity of illegal substances, even as scientists were learning that habitual opium use could shorten life and cause physical and mental problems.

There was at least one other drug frequently used in Southeast Asia at this time. Marijuana, the dried leaves of a type of hemp plant, was less expensive and therefore more popular than opium. It could be grown anywhere, but was easy to plant in rugged mountain areas. The drug, which was smoked in cigarette or tobacco form, was less harmful than opium. But it affected

The results of a 1952 opium raid carried out by the police in Singapore. The man in the center is carrying opium pipes, lamps, and drug containers.

thinking, made the smoker lazy, and was a wasteful and costly habit. Like opium, the more scientists studied it, the less they liked what it did to people.

Well aware of the harmful aspects of opium and marijuana, Malaysian authorities acted. They closed opium dens and made very harsh laws for people who were caught with even small amounts of either drug. Among the punishments for having a small amount of opium or marijuana was a jail term or a beating with a whip or both. The death penalty was enacted for people convicted of having even modest amounts of drugs—about a pound. Several Malaysians—Malays, Chinese, and Indians—were executed, usually by hanging. The imprisonment and death sentence of two Australians found with drugs in 1985 created international attention. Malaysian officials believe that more and more nations are backing their stand against *dadah* (illegal drugs).

Chapter 7

CULTURE SPOKEN,
CULTURE SEEN

More people would enjoy culture if it were as much fun in their country as it is in Malaysia. Culture in many lands means a stuffy look at art, music, dance, and literature. That is not true here. A cultured Malay is one who knows about his or her ancestors. He or she also is aware of the origins of the village, knows where beautiful flowers or healing plants grow, or can tell hundreds of historic legends. A cultured Malay knows all about his or her own people.

SHADOW PLAYS

The flavor of Malay history has for centuries been passed on in the shadow play. This art form involves many puppets made of sticks, hide, wood, or metal. A lantern is placed behind a large screen and the puppets are moved in front of the lantern. The audience sits or stands in front of the screen for hours as a single puppeteer tells stories using dozens of characters. Some puppets are men or women, some are gods, some are animals. But the puppeteer makes them all come alive to talk, dance, fight, marry, die, or fly up to heaven.

Opposite page: Puppets in a shadow play

A puppeteer with some of the puppets he uses for his show

The shadow play, or *wayang kulit,* did not originate in Malaysia. The plays came to the Malays from Indonesia, where Hindus from India brought this entertainment six thousand years ago. Plays carry messages about good behavior, based on religious themes. They no longer have religious meaning to the Muslim Malays, who eagerly await plays at harvest, wedding, and local celebrations, especially along the east coast. Shadow plays survived the Malay conversion to Islam, because Islam did not pass on ancient folktales and the wayang kulit did.

The puppeteer is a one-person show. He or she has memorized dozens of parts in dozens of plays that last for hours. The puppeteer's voice changes as characters come and go. Some even have one or more musical instruments used to highlight the

The batik industry is thriving in Malaysia. Both contemporary (left) and traditional (right) designs are produced.

action. As television spreads to smaller cities, the shadow play is in danger of dying out. That's too bad, because this ancient form of entertainment ties a Malay to his or her past.

BATIK

If the shadow play is dying, batik is alive and well. This colorful cloth was first created in Indonesia. But it is very well made and very popular in Malaysia. In fact, a person wearing a short-sleeve batik shirt or blouse is considered formally dressed in this tropical climate.

Batik is made by creating a pattern with wax on plain cloth. The cloth is dyed with the wax drawing on it, then boiled to remove the wax. This process is repeated to make splashy, bright designs. The wax can be drawn with a pencil or stenciled once or repeatedly onto the cloth. Batik is found in everything from swimsuits to tablecloths. Batik can be found everywhere, but especially in Pinang and Johor Baharu.

Gold and silver threads are used when weaving songket.

WEAVING

A much richer and more expensive cloth can be found on looms in northeast Malaysia. *Songket* combines real gold and silver threads in heavy cloth usually worn only on very special occasions. A yard of the woven fabric can exceed the weekly pay of a Malaysian adult. Malay weddings are the most common places where songket is worn.

Much less expensive are the many products woven from bamboo and other materials. All over the country, in large cities and small villages, handsome baskets, containers, fans, bags, mats, tables, stools, and other furniture are offered for sale. These products are more durable than their thin, greenish-blond strands appear.

A silversmith making filigree jewelry

METALWORK

East coast artists do wonderful work in hammered silver and brass. But pewter, which is 97 percent tin, is used to create cups, plates, vases, salt and pepper shakers, beer mugs—even jewelry. It is the country's most famous metal.

Selangor pewter, named for the state where it is mined, is found in homes all over the world. The bright, silvery metal is formed and polished to a shiny appearance or given a flat (dull) surface. Created not far from Kuala Lumpur, the metal is sculpted by hand and finished by rubbing with smooth or rough leaves.

Classic examples of Malay metalwork are visible in any of the country's many museums. Tough but delicate looking *kris* (knives) were for centuries worn by adult males. These knives have wavy blades and pistol grips. They were seldom used in anger, but were instead a decorative item. A kris today is a very valuable antique.

Two of the many elaborate kinds of kites to be seen in Malaysia

GAMES

Malays have developed several games into art forms. In fact, it is sometimes hard to tell where a craft ends and a game begins. A good example is kite flying. Along the east coast of the peninsula, adults produce vivid kites more than 6 feet (1.8 meters) wide and 4 feet (1.2 meters) high. These kites, which make a buzzing sound in the wind, are flown on weekends and special occasions. Kites from different villages are entered in contests. Different kite owners see who can knock down the others' kites or see who can fly a kite the highest. Kites are so popular that they were chosen as the symbol for MAS, the nation's airline.

Another game involves less skill in construction, but even more skill in playing. That is top spinning. Like kite flying, this is usually done only by older children and adults. Each has a large wooden top wound around with a rope. Tops are sent spinning, just like starting a lawn mower. The object is to see whose top can spin the longest or whose top can knock the other tops over. Malay tops can weigh as much as 15 pounds (6.8 kilograms) and spin for more than an hour.

Sepak raga, a game of skill, is played only with a small ball made of basketlike strips. Players, usually men or boys, get in a circle and keep the ball off the ground using everything but their hands. Feet, knees, elbows, heads, shoulders—anything goes, but hands. When a net is put up and the game takes on rules like volleyball, it is called *sepak takraw*.

DANCES

It is hard to tell where sports stop and dance begins. *Silat* is the Malay answer to karate. It developed on the west coast five hundred years ago as self-defense. Today, silat is performed to music and involves speed and grace, rather than force. Dances of all kinds are common in this country, though the best seem to have come from Thailand. *Makyong* is a romantic dream that includes opera and comedy. There are no stage props, but costumes are colorful and costly. Usually, Thai or Buddhist dances involve women, or men and women. Dances developed elsewhere are usually for men only. Some dancers in Sarawak and Sabah can dance themselves into and out of hypnotic trances.

Dancers from Sarawak (left) and musicians in a
Hindu temple (right) accompanying the chanting of prayers

MUSIC

Music makes dances even more interesting, and Malays have for centuries had orchestras. Most instruments in a Malay orchestra are drums. Gongs, chimes, string instruments, oboes, flutes, and xylophones also can be found in such a group. Royal orchestras, founded hundreds of years ago, play in some states on holidays and are broadcast on the radio.

LITERATURE

Much has been written about Malaysia, but the most famous writing so far has been produced by Europeans. Englishmen Somerset Maugham and Joseph Conrad are just two of many foreigners who have written stories with Malaysian settings. Malaysia's best-known book is *Malay Annals*, written in the fifteenth century. It describes the beginnings of Malacca, starting with legends. Today, books are sold everywhere. Many are religious. They help Malaysians adapt their ancient religions to modern times.

Malaysia has many, many festivals. The Birthday of the Goddess of Mercy, "Kuan Yin" is in July. Celebrants pray for her blessings in her temple, Jalan Pitt, in Pinang (above), where there also is a puppet show.

FESTIVALS

With a multiracial cultural heritage, Malaysia has dozens of local, regional, and national festivals throughout the year. Chinese New Year is celebrated on the first day of the first moon and the traditional New Year's Day, a public holiday, is celebrated on January 1. In spring Hindus and Sikhs celebrate the new year. Many festivals concern harvests, birthdays of important people, and religious events. There are festivals marking the giant turtle season, children's day, and of course, National Day, the anniversary of independence, or *merdeka*, on August 31.

Above: Mount Kinabalu, Sabah, is the highest peak in Malaysia.   Below: The beach at Batu Ferringhi, Pinang, one of the most popular beach resorts in Southeast Asia

Chapter 8

FUN FOR TOURISTS

Three and one-quarter million foreigners visit Malaysia each year. The reasons are obvious—it's easy to get around. A tourist can spend the morning in the mountains, the afternoon at a beach, and the evening in a city. The mixture of old and new, primitive and modern, and wild and tame in a multiracial society with different cultures is too good to pass up.

MOUNTAINS

The nation's highest peak is Mount Kinabalu, a two-hour jet flight east of Kuala Lumpur in the state of Sabah. At 13,431 feet (4,094 meters), it is higher than anything within 1,000 miles (1,609 kilometers) in any direction. Despite its height, there is no snow on this peak. It is just too warm. But the climb is cool and rugged, and the view from the summit can be very nice.

Travelers who want to climb hire a guide. A typical guide is an older woman from one of the local tribes. This lady willingly carries a large pack of food and supplies, even though she may weigh no more than 80 pounds (36 kilograms).

At lower altitudes, the flowers and trees cause the climber to stop and look or take photos. But as the path winds upward, the

trees become shorter and more twisted, and such things as flowers shaped like cups disappear. As the climber nears the peak, there is little but bare rock. Atop Mount Kinabalu, if the clouds break, tourists can see the Sabah coastline, smaller hills and mountains, and look far out into the South China Sea.

RESORTS

There are hundreds of smaller mountains, hills about 5,000 feet (1,524 meters) high, on the mainland. Several are resorts where tourists and Malaysians can escape the intense heat of the lowlands. Temperatures seldom pass 70 degrees Fahrenheit (21 degrees Celsius) and sweaters or jackets are often needed in the evening.

Genting Highlands, a new resort just north of Kuala Lumpur, is 5,814 feet (1,762 meters) high and features a huge gambling casino, night clubs, lavish landscaping, even a bowling alley. Guests can travel from a high-rise hotel to the golf course in a cable car. For families, boat rides on a large artificial lake are popular.

Fraser's Hill resort is only twenty miles (thirty-two kilometers) from Genting, but it is completely different. Created by an Englishman early in the twentieth century, the resort or "station" is 4,777 feet (1,446 meters) high. There is a golf course, swimming pool, and lovely gardens, but Fraser's isn't on a main road and so it is not crowded. Also, the last few miles to its old-fashioned resort are so narrow that traffic takes turns going up and down the hill.

Cameron Highlands, midway between Kuala Lumpur and Pinang, is the oldest and largest hill station. The tallest hill here is

Opposite page: Cameron Highlands Resort

Genting Highlands

6,664 feet (2,030 meters), which means that there are a few more clouds, more rain, and even slightly cooler temperatures. The place has wonderful old, English-style cottages, farms where tea and flowers are raised for sending all over the world, plus the usual golf course and hotels. The well-marked jungle walks here are a treat.

Much lower, Pinang Hill nevertheless offers escape from the heat, if only by a few degrees. There is no road, but a cable car hauls visitors slowly up the 3,000 feet (914 meters). There are nice homes along the railway, and at the top there is a hotel, a Muslim mosque, a Hindu temple, lovely gardens, and a breathtaking view. Watching the lights come on each evening in George Town from the hill is one of Asia's great delights.

Kota Tinggi is the lowest and least well-known hill resort. It is also the most Malay, and can be a great deal of fun. Kota Tinggi is

Left: A ferryboat carries passengers between Pinang Island and the mainland.   Right: Colorful sailboats at Batu Ferringhi

east of Johor Baharu in the thinly populated southeast corner of the country. The hill is just 2,000 feet (609 meters), but there are gentle waterfalls, natural pools for swimming and, on weekends, lots of Malaysians. No fancy hotels are here, but there are numerous camping chalets.

Malaysia's oldest hill resort is also the hardest to reach. Maxwell Hill, north of Ipoh, can only be entered in an off-road vehicle, which meets visitors near the bottom of a winding, narrow road that climbs about 2,000 feet (609 meters). Very quiet and peaceful, Maxwell has lovely gardens and serves traditional tea amid these green and growing colors. There are a number of small cottages, and the west coast can be seen from some of them on a clear day.

ISLANDS

Many people think of islands when they think of the tropics and Malaysia has several worth a visit.

Tioman Island, four hours by boat off the east coast, is a skin diver's paradise. There are beautiful beaches and rugged coral formations in safe and shallow water. There is a large, resort hotel set on a very white beach. Behind it are two mountains surrounded by dense jungle. First visited thousands of years ago by sailors for its fresh waters, Tioman has been used in movies when a beautiful South Seas island setting is needed.

Far, far to the northwest are the Langkawi Islands. They are several hours by boat north of Pinang and, because of their distance, aren't frequently visited. To encourage tourists, the government recently made the Langkawi group a free port. Visitors can buy anything on the islands and not pay taxes. There are beautiful beaches, a freshwater pool, hiking and motorbike trails, and just thirty thousand residents spread among all these islands. As a result, swimmers often find they have an entire beach all to themselves.

Midway between Kuala Lumpur and Pinang, off the west coast, is Pangkor Island. This is a major resort destination for people living in Kuala Lumpur, and there is a good road to it from Ipoh. Crowded on weekends and holidays, the island is a brief ferry ride from the mainland. One of the nice things about Pangkor is how friendly everyone is. Another nicety is that it is small—a walk around the entire island can be done in an afternoon. But whenever the heat overcomes a hiker, he or she can take a quick dip.

Pinang, Malaysia's largest island, is now linked to the mainland by a huge new bridge. The north side of the island has pretty beaches and a string of hotels set amid shady palms. To the west are hilly spice plantations, then fields of rice and other grains. Pleasant villages can be found along the coast and inland in the

Left: A tourist hotel on the beach of Pinang at dusk
Right: Palms in the jungle

south, with George Town's best temples in suburbs on the
southeast. Buses, taxis, and rental cars are available for round-the-
island trips, a distance of thirty-five miles (fifty-six kilometers).

JUNGLES

The last frontiers on earth may be the jungles of Asia, Africa,
and South America. Perhaps that is why there are so many
foreigners who want to see them. The best way to see thick and
potentially dangerous jungle in Malaysia is by boat. Many rivers
cut through Taman Negara National Park and other jungle areas,
and camping on a sand spit is a tidy way to enjoy the various
sights and sounds. This sort of adventure is an important source
of income to tribal people, who act as guides and boat handlers.

A tea plantation

Chapter 9

THE VARIETY OF
MALAYSIA

RURAL AREAS

Much of rural Malaysia is a living travel poster. Swaying palms above a silver stretch of sandy, deserted beach, gently lapping surf, a warm, tropical sun—such places still exist. For other tastes, there are other scenes. Hill villages, called stations, are 5,000 feet (1,524 meters) or more above sea level. They feature cool and misty breezes, rare flowers in bloom all year long, fresh strawberries for breakfast, and tea plantations that separate one misty, green hill from the next. Or there are primitive jungles with coffee-colored rivers and people who still hunt with blowpipes.

VILLAGES

A typical village has three thousand or fewer residents and is on a narrow, two-lane asphalt road or highway. The main street has two-story buildings, most often operated by persons of Chinese descent. These stucco or cement-block groceries, motorbike dealerships, restaurants, or hardware stores are open in front, since the weather is always warm. The family lives above in several rooms. They sell goods purchased from local farmers or delivered by trucks or vans that may be thirty years old and British, or shiny-new and Japanese or German.

Malays living in villages or near their fields have for centuries favored a unique style of house. The home is built on stilts so that residents are bothered neither by occasional high water nor by wild animals. The house is made of stained or painted wood and has three or four rooms with windows and portals, but no glass and no doors. These openings—and the slight elevation—take advantage of whatever cool breeze may exist. Carved shutters are closed when the family is away. The roof is ornately decorated and hangs far enough over the sides of the house to keep out rain.

Cross streets run a block or two on either side of the main road before turning into country. The kind of countryside depends on where the village is. To the north on the peninsula's east and west coasts, the land is mostly rice paddies. The lower west side of the peninsula is devoted to growing rubber or palm trees.

Outside the villages, near any coast, dozens of prahus are anchored. These brightly painted, wooden boats bob out to sea each day in search of fish, a staple of the Malaysian diet.

RURAL AREAS IN SARAWAK AND SABAH

Rural areas in Sarawak and Sabah are different from anywhere else. The people, who may be members of the Iban, Dyak, or other tribes, practice slash-and-burn agriculture. A field is used until it is no longer fertile. Then they saw and burn down space in nearby jungle for a new field. Tribe members live on rice, root crops, fish, and wild game. They trade produce for items not readily available—sugar, salt, and coffee. But their homes are unique.

Left: A Dyak demonstrating the use of a blowpipe
Right: A communal house in Sarawak

Many Borneo residents live in longhouses. An entire settlement with dozens of families may live in a single such longhouse. There is one very long common room with private rooms for each family beside it. The common room, where children play and adults chat, may stretch for fifty yards (forty-six meters). A corrugated metal roof covers the entire building, with outbuildings nearby. One form of decor inside many longhouses is unusual: there are still skulls on display from when the tribespeople were headhunters.

NORTHERN AREAS

There are even more primitive people amid the northern mountains on the mainland. Orang asli, original men, are racially mixed and poorly adapted for life in a modern nation. They wear little or no clothing, hunt with crude bows and arrows or blowpipes, use stone tools, and gather much of their food instead of growing it. Their homes are little more than shacks made of fallen leaves. The government protects these people from outsiders, but offers them schools and better housing on the edge of the jungle. Though things are changing for them, the orang asli remain one of the most primitive groups on earth.

Several years ago Malaysia's northern border, facing Thailand, was heavily guarded by soldiers and police. Along a 360-mile (579-kilometer) road running from one coast to the other, there were bunkers covered with sandbags. Machine guns, rifles, and other weapons could be seen in these fortified positions. Officials claimed the armed men were guarding against Communist guerrillas. However, some residents believed there were not enough Communists in the country to worry about. Residents believed the soldiers were really looking for smugglers.

Smugglers, at that time, brought in many items from Thailand, everything from food to jewels to drugs. Food was very cheap in Thailand, so Malaysians went there to try to sneak rice back across the border. There were professional smugglers who ran drugs. The government was mainly interested in them.

These days, there is much argument about what may be being smuggled, from drugs to weapons, and about what countries might be supplying the goods and profiting from the smuggling. Foreign governments accused of participating deny this.

Malaysians visit Thailand because prices are low and because beaches in that country are very nice. Thais come to Malaysia for several reasons. They have been known to steal big cars on Pinang Island, then drive them over the border, never to be seen again.

MAJOR CITIES

Malaysia's major cities are linked by paved roads, an adequate rail system, and numerous airlines. It is sometimes even possible to make an entrance by ferry or pleasure boat.

Kuala Lumpur has well-planned streets, expressways, and parks.
Many other stretches of green add beauty to the city.

KUALA LUMPUR

The nation's capital is halfway between Singapore and the Thai border, a few miles in from the west coast. Kuala Lumpur, usually called K. L., now has more than a million people and is a mix of older neighborhoods and startlingly modern high-rise buildings. Founded where two rivers, the Klang and the Gombak, meet on their way to the sea, the capital has grown in every direction since it was just another noisy tin mining village one hundred years ago.

Kuala Lumpur has thousands of cars, trucks, and motorcycles, yet it isn't the clogged mass of polluted humanity found in some Asian countries. One reason is because modern planning has gone into streets and highways. Second, there are large parks, playing fields, and other green and growing recreation areas. A third reason is unusual in Asia: overpopulation is not yet a problem.

Kuala Lumpur

K. L. has enough public housing and there are jobs for most people who live in such large apartment buildings. Many Malaysians work as government employees. They perform jobs such as police, office workers, gardeners, guards, cleaners, guides, and more. A walk along the Klang River starting at the old railway station presents the old and the new in this city. On the left is the National Mosque, a modern contrast to the old-style rail station. Loudspeakers boom the voice of the muezzin in this area where the city began. Straight ahead is the General Post Office, a building so white and new it seems to glow in the tropical sunlight. Malaysians inherited good postal service from the British and have maintained it. All over the country, men and women in handsome tan uniforms with red trim deliver mail daily.

To the right is a Hindu temple. The aroma of flowers swirls around the worshipers and their even more colorful idols. On ahead are streets where Hindu and Muslim shopkeepers sell goods from India. Romantic music on a tape played at full volume, plus the strong smell of spice, and rows of pretty *saris* (dresses) tell us we are in the Indian quarter.

Surrounded by tall buildings, Chinatown's squat, two-story shophouses haven't changed much in a century. Whiffs of tea, fish, smoked duck, onions, incense, and fragrant wood float among shoppers and shopkeepers. They all appear to be in constant motion. The people here love to yell to each other as they work. They stay up quite late. Many Malaysians, especially the Chinese, eat their evening meal as late as midnight.

As if to prove that K. L. offers variety, a Church of England cathedral can be seen to the right and another mosque is off to the left.

Also on the left is a group of government buildings, all of them

*Three views of Kuala Lumpur: the confluence of the Klang
and Gombak rivers (top), an ultramodern shopping mall (below right),
and a bank built in a more traditional style (below left)*

ornate, where crafts from throughout Malaysia are on display and for sale. Across the street is the Selangor Club. This club has a cricket field, where English plantation owners once sat in the shade and were fanned with palm leaves by their servants. The busy *jalan*, or street, here is named for Abdul Rahman, Malaysia's first prime minister.

Hotels, restaurants, shops, and movie theaters line the street. In the Malay section, there is a modern shopping center to the left, with clothes designed in Europe but made in Malaysia and elsewhere in Asia. Here, the sidewalk becomes shops for one-person businesses—street peddlers. These hard-working people sell everything from shoes to hats, from keys to souvenirs, from holy books to sticky snacks. Pedestrians have a choice. They can either walk carefully among the umbrellas that shade these sidewalk salespeople, or walk in the street and dodge traffic.

Shopping for food is quite easy. Much food is purchased and consumed on the street, but many apartments have small refrigerators where meat and other cold or frozen food can be stored. The special Sunday Market is a night market, but it takes place on Saturday night. At the market, special Malay food and bargains ranging from antiques to wild T-shirts and trendy tennis shoes can be found. This is a popular weekend spot.

K. L. has more attractions. Huge hotels and embassies of most of the world's countries line shady streets. Horses race on a beautiful track that is covered with thick grass. The national museum is a great place to spend a hot afternoon. So are major shopping centers, where the air conditioning is a shock after walking in 'from the noonday heat. Like many new buildings, the shopping centers are so cool they feel like big refrigerators. In all, K. L. has become a modern city in amazingly few years.

Left: Some local transportation   Right: Stairway leading up to Batu Caves

Beyond the big buildings are blue-green hills. Here are the Batu
Caves, discovered just a century ago in a huge limestone cliff.
Many activities go on nearby, including tin mining, rubber tree
and vegetable growing, and various crafts, such as making pewter
handicrafts and dyeing special cloth.

West of the city is Petaling Jaya, a huge suburb that is
Malaysia's only planned city so far. It has 250,000 people, mostly
Chinese Malaysians who work in one of the nearly two hundred
factories that have sprung up here since independence. To the
north are two mountain resorts, Genting Highlands and Fraser's
Hill. And in between are a zoo, a special jungle peak, and large,
commercial amusements. Modern buses and taxis whisk K. L.
residents out here and back every day.

Kuala Lumpur

Malacca

MALACCA

If Kuala Lumpur is the future, Malacca is the past. Malaysians realize the importance of preserving the old and that is why Malacca is such a pleasant place today. This city of about 100,000 population is 90 miles (145 kilometers) southwest of Kuala Lumpur and 150 miles (241 kilometers) northwest of Singapore.

Everything about the town urges relaxation and sightseeing. On a hill overlooking the city are the ruins of a fort and, a bit higher up, a church. These buildings were constructed by Portuguese sailors more than 450 years ago and have withstood attacks by enemies and tropical heat. The breeze up here is constant and trees and monuments provide a bit of shade.

Down the hills are several buildings in pink brick or red clay. They were built by the Dutch, who were replaced by the English, but left a thick-walled church and city hall for use by today's Malaysians. Across the nearby Malacca River, which is brown with mud, are two narrow streets. This section of town is the oldest Chinese settlement in Malaysia. Two words represent these people, known as the Straits Chinese: *baba* and *nonya*.

Babas are male Chinese and nonyas are females. Together, these hard-working people came from southern China with no money but with a great deal of hope. They took lowly jobs and saved, gaining enough to buy small businesses and educate their children. Businesses grew and the Straits Chinese began to enjoy the results of their labor. Their homes took on a beautiful blend of Chinese and Malay living. Everything from furniture to food showed influences of both cultures. Having lived in Malaysia for several generations, the baba and nonya Chinese became less attached to China and more a unique culture of their own. Costly

*A shopping street in Malacca (left), and some buildings
erected by the Dutch (right)*

Chinese silks, for example, became clothing with fascinating
Malay designs. Nowhere is this combination more prized than in
nonya cooking.

There are other Chinese influences all around Malacca. Bukit
China is a very old, hilly cemetery. The first graves were dug here
only a few years after the arrival of the Chinese sailors, more than
five hundred years ago. The Buddhist temple known as Cheng
Hoong Teng is the oldest in the country. Movie theaters show
bright banners advertising Chinese movies, made in Hong Kong,
but quite popular here. The country's best antique shops are here,
too. Most of them are Chinese operated, but feature items from
English, Dutch, and Portuguese rule.

The Malacca River

The only living reminders of the Portuguese in Malacca can be found just south of the city. A small village of descendants of the invaders live just like any other Malaysians. Their homes are elevated, men wear shorts and T-shirts and women wear colorful, cool skirts or dresses. No one here can remember much Portuguese. These farmers or fishermen or small business people may look European, but their ancestors long ago decided to follow the Southeast Asian way of life. They remain staunchly Catholic and celebrate Christian holidays along with the various Muslim, Buddhist, and Hindu special occasions.

IPOH

This is the capitol of the state of Perak. Perak has two million people, more than any other state, and is a miniature Malaysia. It has seashore, mountains, rice paddies in the north, and

A tin mine

plantations in the south. A rich source of hardwood, Perak is the
center of tin mining, too. Just south of Ipoh are limestone caves,
many of them Buddhist and Hindu temples. From one of these
caves a visitor can look out into an almost prehistoric valley,
surrounded by hills. Caves provide the only easy way in or out.

Ipoh, on the main road north of Kuala Lumpur, is a large,
hurried city. In fact, the main road skirts the downtown area,
which is almost exclusively Malaysian Chinese and always busy.
The city has a well-cared-for look and is on the banks of two
rivers, the Kinta and the Pari. Several millionaires live in Ipoh.
These men are tin mine owners who made vast amounts of money

and live in large, stylish stucco houses. They drive Mercedes-Benz and other large cars and most still work, though they could relax.

This is Malaysia's most Chinese city. The Chinese may seem alike to a foreigner, yet they consider themselves very different. Malaysian Chinese may have relatives in Canton or in other parts of southern China. Seafaring Hokkiens came here, many from an island called Hainan. Swatow is another part of south China where Malaysian forebears lived. A few may even have come from Shanghai, on the east coast, or from the nation's capital, Peking (now called Beijing), farther north. Many Chinese Malaysians are Straits Chinese with little or no ties to the mainland. But those with ties like to remember their ancestors.

GEORGE TOWN

The country's second largest city has 400,000 or more people and is often called by the wrong name. George Town is on the resort island of Pinang, off the northwest coast of mainland Malaysia. Many people who go to the island believe it and its large city share the same name. Not so.

"Everything is better on Pinang," laughed a librarian in Kuala Lumpur. "There's always a breeze, the city is nice, the island is pretty and the food is the very best. Here in Kuala Lumpur, when they want to say something is very good, they call it 'Pinang style.'"

Indeed, the smell of food is around every corner in George Town. One of the most popular sundown spots is on Gurney Drive, where a seawall stretches for a mile or more in front of huge old homes. Here is where cooks gather, selling wonderful treats to whomever pulls up in a car or strolls by.

Above: Looking across George Town toward the harbor
Below: The clock tower of George Town (left) and the city's Komtar Building (right),
which is Pinang's largest shopping complex.

Above: A trishaw carrying passengers
Below: The shopping area of Chinatown in George Town (left) and a market in Kuala Terengganu (right) selling red rambutans (in the center of stall)

There is more than food here, though. This historic city has a pastel clock tower, a new department store-office complex that towers over the town, an ultramodern bridge running from the island to the mainland, and twenty-four-hour car and passenger ferry service. There are enough narrow, dark, and mysterious side streets to please anyone who wants to see the Orient as it used to be. George Town is a kaleidoscope of dining, bargain hunting, and people watching. Among the more interesting people to watch are recent or longtime residents who came from India.

Anything that can be said about Malaysian Indians proves to be a contradiction. For every wealthy jeweler or gold dealer, there is a penniless trishaw (three-wheel bicycle) driver. For every lavishly dressed woman, there is a ragged woman selling a few vegetables on the street. For almost every Hindu, there is a Muslim. All this makes Indians in George Town and elsewhere especially fascinating. Even though they are a minority everywhere in Malaysia, their influence has been great.

KUALA TERENGGANU

Ipoh is very Chinese, George Town is a wonderful mix, and Kuala Terengganu, on the east coast of the peninsula, is Malay.

Built where the Terengganu River meets the sea, this city has a colorful fishing fleet of wooden boats. These boats, known among sailors for their quality, are made in villages on islands in the river. On any day, passenger ferries visit these sandy islands, picking up people who work in Kuala Terengganu and dropping those from the city who build boats. Where there are boats, there are fishermen and Kuala Terengganu is no exception. Dozens of kinds of fresh fish are unloaded in the market daily.

Above: A street in Kota Kinabalu, Sabah, with apartments
above street-level shops   Below: Kuching, Sarawak (left)
and the Abu Bakar Mosque in Johor (right)

Traffic in Kota Baharu

The pace here is noticeably slower, from the speed of traffic to the smaller number of motorcycles that buzz in all Malaysian cities. Beaches are longer and cleaner on the east coast, even though large oil refineries are in operation. Only recently has there been a road that travels the entire coast. The road is opening up a very Malay, very Muslim, and very traditional area to tourists by the thousands. Large hotels and big tour buses don't seem to bother east coast residents. No matter how fast tourists operate, chances are they will slow down here.

OTHER CITIES

Several other towns and cities are equally interesting. Kota Baharu, far to the northeast, is the site where the Japanese landed in 1941. It is very near Thailand, and has ancient mosques and Thai temples. Johor Baharu, across a bridge from Singapore, is a state capital with handsome gardens and estates. Kuching, 400 miles (708 kilometers) east in Sarawak, has more that 100,000 residents and is the biggest city on Borneo. Kota Kinabalu, in Sabah, is a jumping-off point for mountain climbing and jungle walks. It is safe to say that no country this size has more variety.

Above: A baby rests comfortably in a hammock in the center of the family group.
Below: A semiconductor scientist (left) and a farmer weeding his crops (right)

Chapter 10

EVERYDAY LIFE

Weekends mean different days to different people in this country. Half of the states devote the period from noon Thursday through Friday as the weekend, since Friday is the traditional Muslim holy day. Friday also is the day Hindus are most likely to visit their temples. The other states look at the weekend from noon Saturday through the end of the day on Sunday. Luckily, most shops selling consumer goods are open every day from 9:00 or 10:00 A.M. to 9:00 P.M. Offices hours are usually 9:00 A.M. to 5:00 P.M.

How can the modern Malaysian be described? The typical resident of a town or village is of Malay descent, a Muslim, able to read and speak the national language, the owner of a motorbike who may soon purchase a car, and a homeowner living in an elevated, four-room house with electricity but no plumbing. He or she is a fairly young person, perhaps twenty-eight or twenty-nine years old. This Malaysian is the parent of three or four children, has a garden, owns a radio, and has a savings account.

The father in the family may be a farmer, a laborer, or have some sort of service job. His wife is expected to care for the home and the children, to shop each day for fresh food, and to prepare meals.

Left: Traditionally Malays eat with their fingers
Right: Satay, served with a small dish of spicy sauce

FOOD

A typical Malay meal is eaten only with the right hand—no knives, forks, spoons, or chopsticks are used. Food is served on banana leaves or plates and might include rice or noodles in a spicy sauce with beef, chicken, fish, and vegetables. Or, Malaysia's most famous dish, *satay*, might be served. Satay are bite-sized pieces of chicken, lamb, or beef on thin spears of bamboo. They are dipped in a light batter and then cooked over a charcoal fire. These tasty bits of meat are dipped in spicy peanut sauce. Frequently, a salad of cucumbers and fruit is served, too. The evening meal is usually eaten after sundown, which occurs throughout the year around 7:00 P.M.

A display of food in a market in downtown Kuala Lumpur

Nonya food mixes the great variety of ingredients found in southern Chinese food with the spicy tastes all Malays enjoy. As good as the food is, there is one catch—it is served in almost all Straits Chinese homes, but is hard to find in a restaurant. That is because the Straits Chinese have been established in other kinds of businesses over the years. A nonya meal might include prawns (giant shrimp) cooked in spicy coconut milk, fried noodles with bits of onion and pepper, slices of cooling cucumber to help overcome the tangy food, and a pot of hot tea. No more than half a dozen restaurants in all of Malaysia serve nonya food, but it is eaten every day in many Straits Chinese homes.

Public school students

EDUCATION

England is frequently credited with Malaysia's superior public schools, but much of the credit must go to Prime Minister Rahman, who saw to it that students nationwide were taught the same subjects at the same grade levels. Today, all young Malaysians receive at least nine and frequently eleven years of public or private education, attending school forty weeks each year. They learn the official Bahasa Malaysia language, plus whatever second language is emphasized in their school. Depending on the village and whether the school is private or public, the second language can be Mandarin Chinese, Tamil or Bengali (Indian dialects), or English. There are seven universities, an institute of technology, and several teacher-training colleges and vocational centers.

LANGUAGE

Bahasa Malaysia, the official language, is spoken by all younger Malaysians of all races and many older residents. It is much easier to learn than any Chinese dialect. That is because Malaysian pronunciations are easy. For example, there are no tongue-twisting tricks or sing-song tone changes. It is a pleasant language to hear, too. Spoken on the street, the words are often mixed with English. This same language is spoken in much of Indonesia and in parts of the Philippines.

Bahasa Malaysia is the most popular modern version of an ancient language. The language comes from the South Pacific and is not related to any Chinese or Indian speech. At least 160 million people currently speak this exotic tongue.

TRANSPORTATION

The road system in West Malaysia is extensive and about the best in Southeast Asia. In Sabah and Sarawak, roads are not very good. The most common form of transportation in Malaysia is by road, but it isn't for the fainthearted. There are a few miles of multilane highway, toll roads just south of Kuala Lumpur, that may be the best in Asia. Elsewhere, log trucks, bicycles, turbocharged sedans, and motorbikes share narrow roads—with cattle, goats, and children. Driving is on the left-hand, or British, side of the road.

Buses are common ways to move from one city to another. So is the rail system, which serves the west coast of the peninsula. A second line runs diagonally north from Kuala Lumpur, allowing views of Taman Negara National Park and the northeast. There

A Malaysian Airlines 737 at Kota Baharu airport (left)
and the railway station in Kuala Lumpur (right)

are three classes of rail travel. All first-class and some second-class coaches are air conditioned. First-class stops only at major cities; other classes stop at every village along the line. Top speed of the trains is less than fifty miles (eighty kilometers) an hour. First-class time from Singapore to K. L. is six hours, while second- and third-class runs take about ten hours.

River transportation is important in East Malaysia, where the roads are not very good. Air transport has grown rapidly. Malaysian Airline System (MAS), which was established in 1971, serves as both an international and domestic airline.

SPORTS AND RECREATION

Between the end of work and the evening meal, men gather to talk and may play sepak takraw, a game like volleyball that involves keeping a small, wicker ball in the air. No hands are permitted, but every other part of the body is used to kick or bump the ball back and forth over a net. Other games played in villages include badminton, at which Malaysians are highly

Faces of Malaysia

skilled. Badminton competition among Asian countries is intense. The Malay badminton team won a medal at the 1992 summer Olympics in Barcelona, Spain.

The world's most popular sport, soccer, is a Malaysian favorite followed closely in newspapers, TV, and radio. Other sports covered by the media include squash, golf, karate, motorcycle and car racing, and bicycle racing. Along the east coast men hold top-spinning and kite-flying contests which attract tourists. On Borneo, several tribes are expert horsemen.

TODAY'S MALAYSIAN

When a Malaysian isn't playing, dining, fixing a meal, or working, he or she is engaged in quiet conversation. The average Malaysian has a good grasp of his country's politics. World affairs also are discussed. A modern Malaysian is comfortable talking to an elder about the old days while a cassette recorder blasts out a pop song by one of dozens of nationally known singers and musicians.

115

MAP KEY

Alor Setar	D2	Lahid Datu	D5
Banguey (island)	D5	Lundu	E3
Belaga	E4	Lutong	E4
Beluran	D5	Malacca, Strait of	E1, E2
Bintulu	E4	Marudi	E4
Brunei Bay	D4, E4	Melaka (Malacca)	E2
Butterworth	D2	Mersing	E2
Daro	E4	Miri	E4
Darvel Bay	E5	Mukah	E4
Dickson, Port	E2	Pahang (river)	E2
George Town (Pinang)	D2	Pekan	E2
Ipoh	E2	Pinang (island)	D2
Iran Mtns. (mountains)	E4, E5	Rajung (river)	E4
Johor Baharu	E2	Sabah	D5, E5
Kabong	E4	Sandakan	D5
Kalabakan	E5	Sarawak	E4
Kapit	E4	Seremban	E2
Kelang	E2	Sibu	E4
Keluang	E2	Sibutu Passage	E5
Kinabalu, Mt. (mountain)	D5	Simanggang	E4
Kota Baharu	D2	Simunjan	E4
Kota Kinabalu	D5	Sirik, C. (cape)	E4
Kuala Lipis	E2	Tahan (mountain)	E2
Kuala Lumpur	E2	Taiping	E2
Kuala Terengganu	D2	Tampasak	D5
Kuantan	E2	Tawau	E5
Kuching	E4	Telok Anson	E2
Kudat	D5	Tenggaron, Point	E2
Labuan I. (island)	D5	Upper Kapuas Mts. (mountains)	E4
Labuk Bay	D5	Victoria	D5
		Weston	D5

MINI-FACTS AT A GLANCE

GENERAL INFORMATION

Official Name: Malaysia (in Malay, *Persekutuan Tanah Melayu*)

Capital: Kuala Lumpur

Official Language: Bahasa Malaysia, a form of Malay, is the official language. However, English, Chinese (many dialects), and various Indian dialects are spoken among the many ethnic minorities. Natives of Sarawak and Sabah (formerly East Malaysia) also speak several unwritten languages, particularly Iban.

Government: Malaysia is a federation of thirteen states and one federal territory, Kuala Lumpur, which is governed by a constitutional monarchy and a parliament. The parliament consists of a senate *(Dewan Negara)* and a house of representatives *(Dewan Rakyat)*.

A "supreme ruler," or *yang di-pertuan agong*, serves as a nonpolitical head of the federal government, and is elected for a five-year term from among nine hereditary state rulers. His powers are largely ceremonial. He formally "appoints" the prime minister who is previously determined through election to head the ruling party, and is responsible for protecting the special rights of Malays as well as the legitimate interests of non-Malays. On the prime minister's advice, the yang di-pertuan agong also appoints the other cabinet ministers. The prime minister and the cabinet make and implement government policies.

Hereditary rulers, usually called *sultans*, head nine of Malaysia's state governments. Federally appointed governors head the other four states and federal territories. Each state has its own constitution, a single-house legislature elected by popular vote, and an executive council.

Generally, the federal government is responsible for foreign affairs, defense, internal security, administration of justice (except for matters involving Islamic or native law), federal citizenship, finance, commerce, industry, communications, and transportation. State governments handle immigration and customs matters, development of natural resources and land, local administration, public works, and matters involving Islamic law or Malay customs.

Flag: A yellow crescent and star lie on a blue background in the upper-left corner of the flag. The crescent represents Islam and the fourteen stars represent the thirteen original states and the federal government, as do the flag's fourteen red and white stripes.

National Anthem: Negara Ky ("My Country, My Native Land")

Religion: Islam is established by the constitution as the national religion, but the rights of all religious are also constitutionally protected. To be Malay is to be Muslim. The Malaysian Chinese are primarily Buddhist, yet some Chinese are followers of Taoism, Confucianism, or Christianity.

The Indian population tends to practice Hinduism. Unlike Muslims, Hindus believe in innumerable gods.

Money: Malaysia's central bank, Bank Negara Malaysia, issues Malaysia's basic monetary unit, the ringgit. The ringgit is divided into 100 sen. One U.S. dollar equals 2.60 ringgits as of June 1994.

Weights and Measures: Malaysia uses the metric system.

Population: 19,564,000 (1994 estimate); distribution: 47 percent urban, 53 percent rural. Density: 142 persons per sq. mi.; 55 per km². More than 80 percent of the population live in Peninsular Malaysia (formerly West Malaysia), on the continent. Sarawak and Sabah (formerly East Malaysia) are on the island of Borneo.
　　The population is a mix of ethnic groups, each with its own languages, customs, and life-styles. Overall, Malays account for about 50 percent of the population, Chinese about 35 percent, and Indians (originally from India, including Pakistan) about 10 percent. Numerous other small ethnic groups and tribal subgroups in Sarawak and Sabah make up the remainder of the population.

Cities:

Kuala Lumpur	1,103,200
Ipoh	300,727
Pinang (George Town)	250,578
Johor Baharu	249,880

(Population of Kuala Lumpur based on 1985 estimate; all others, 1980 census)

GEOGRAPHY

Highest point: Mount Kinabalu, 13,431 ft. (4,094 m), in the northeast part of Sabah

Lowest point: Sea level along the coast

Rivers: Due to year-round rainfall, there is perennial stream flow throughout Malaysia, although water levels do fluctuate. The longest river in Peninsular Malaysia is the Pahang (270 mi.;435 km). The Rajung River in Sarawak and Sabah is 350 mi. (563 km) long. Other major rivers include: the Kelantan and Perak in Peninsular Malaysia and the Kinabatangan in Sarawak and Sabah.
　　Historically, rivers have provided an important means of transportation and communication between coastal areas and the interior.

Mountains: Peninsular Malaysia is largely mountainous, with six north-south aligned mountain ranges extending down the center of the peninsula. The 800-mi. (1,287-km) Main Range dominates the region with elevations to 7,000 ft. (2,100 m).
　　Mountains divide Sarawak and Sabah from Indonesian Borneo and include the two highest peaks in the country: Mount Kinabalu in Sabah and Mount Murad in Sarawak.

Climate: On both the peninsula and Sarawak and Sabah the climate is tropical and is strongly influenced by the northeast (November-March) and southwest (June-October) monsoons, high temperatures, heavy rainfall, and high humidity.
　　Average rainfall is 100 in. (254 cm) in Peninsular Malaysia and 150 in. (381 cm) in Sarawak and Sabah.
　　The average year-round temperature is 77 to 80° F. (25 to 26.7° C) in the coastal lowlands and 72 to 83° F. (22.2 to 28.3° C) in interior mountainous areas.

Area: 127,317 sq. mi. (320,749 km²). Peninsular Malaysia: 50,806 sq. mi. (131,588 km²); Sarawak and Sabah: 76,511 sq. mi. (198,161 km²).

Peninsular Malaysia occupies the southern half of the continental Malay peninsula and borders Thailand on the north, Singapore on the south, the Strait of Malacca on the west, and the South China Sea on the east. Sarawak and Sabah occupy the northwestern part of the island of Borneo and are bordered on the north and west by the South China Sea, on the east by the Celebes Sea, and on the south by the province of Borneo.

Peninsular Malaysia and Sarawak and Sabah are physically separated by about 400 mi. (644 km) of the South China Sea.

NATURE

Trees: Malaysia's hot, humid, wet climate provides fertile growing conditions for trees and plants. Approximately 75 percent of Malaysia is covered by dense tropical forest. Huge evergreen rain forests cover at least one-half of the land in Peninsular Malaysia and about three-fourths of the land in Sarawak and Sabah. Mangrove and palm trees flourish in swampy, coastal forests. There are at least 2,500 other types of fruit and hardwood trees, including: fig, mahogany, teak, camphor, ebony, sandalwood, rubber, and bamboo. Coconut palm, durian, guava, papaya, and banana trees are often planted near people's homes.

Generally, undergrowth is poorly developed due to the dense forests that allow little sunlight to penetrate.

Plants: Malaysia is home to one of the largest varieties of flora in the world. Some 8,000 species of lush, flowering plants can be found.

Animals: Numerous types of wildlife can be found throughout Malaysia, including: gibbons (small, tailless, arboreal apes), elephants, tapirs, civets, tigers, anteaters, panthers, rats, and wild pigs. Numerous varieties of monkeys can be found.

On Sarawak and Sabah live orangutans, two-horned rhinoceros, honey bears, and the proboscis monkey.

Various species of poisonous and nonpoisonous snakes, lizards, and crocodiles abound.

Malaysia also is host to the largest and most varied bird population in the world, as well as to over 900 species of butterflies. Insects commonly found include: cockroaches, ants, beetles, scorpions, and leeches.

Fish: On beaches along the Malaysian coasts, green sea turtles and giant leatherback turtles nest regularly.

A variety of fish, along with prawns, crabs, squid, and octopus can be found also.

EVERYDAY LIFE

Holidays and Festivals
(The Islamic calendar moves forward—as opposed to the Gregorian calendar, which only adds one day in leap year—about ten days a year. Therefore, dates for some changeable Islamic holidays are given for 1988.)

January 1, New Year's Day (except Johor, Kadah, Perlis, and Terengganu)

February 1, Federal Territory Day
January/February, Chinese New Year (2 days)
April, Easter Sunday
April, Hindu New Year
May 1, Malaysia Labor Day
May 17-18 (1988), Hari Raya Puasa (marks the end of Ramadan, the fasting month for Muslims; 2 days)
May 30 (in 1988), Wesak Day (Buddha's Birthday)
June 1, Supreme Head of State's Birthday
July 24 (in 1988), Hari Raya Haji (commemorates the Muslim pilgrimage season)
August 14 (in 1988), First Day of Muharram (Islamic New Year)
August 31, Merdeka Day (Independence Day)
October 23 (in 1988), Prophet Muhammad's Birthday
November 8 (in 1988), Deepavali (Indian New Year)
December 25, Christmas

Food: The Malaysian diet is based on rice *(padi)*, which is typically served with meat, fish, a fish sauce, fruit, or vegetables. Numerous tropical fruits and vegetables are eaten regularly, including bananas, mangos, jackfruit, papayas, pineapple, rambutan, and starfruit.

Malaysia's most famous dish is *satay*—small pieces of chicken, lamb, or beef cooked on thin bamboo skewers and eaten with a spicy peanut sauce.

The evening meal is usually eaten after sundown, but the Chinese often eat around midnight.

Housing: Most rural Malays live in settlements called *kampongs*. Kampongs are communities of individual dwellings on stilts, which are erected next to waterways, beaches, roads, or footpaths. These houses were traditionally made of wood with thatch roofs called *atap* (woven palm leaves), and are surrounded by fruit trees. Today most new houses are built of cement and other "modern" materials.

Rural Chinese tend to cluster along roads rather than waterways and live in individual houses built at ground level. Well-to-do and middle-income urban Chinese live in downtown, modern, high-rise apartments; in "shophouses" where they live behind or above their stores; or in suburban homes. Lower-income Chinese, as well as urban Malays and Indians, typically reside in overcrowded run-down, inner-city tenements.

Many rural Indians work on rubber plantations and live in small cottages on the plantation grounds.

Sport and Recreation: Soccer, badminton, and horse racing are the most popular spectator sports. Participatory sports include: cricket, tennis, golf, basketball, squash, table tennis, karate, and motorcycle and bicycle racing. Top-spinning and kite-flying contests are frequent.

Several resorts are popular escapes from the hot temperatures of the lowland areas.

Culture: Folk dances, puppet dramas, traditional handicrafts, and decorative arts are the principal Malaysian art forms. Painting and sculpture are poorly developed, primarily because Islam discourages depiction of humans and animals.

Malay decorative arts include batik cloth, basketry, silver and brasswork, wood carving, and woven bamboo products.

In Sarawak and Sabah, handicrafts are common: handwoven textiles, rattan mats and basketry, woodworking, Selangor pewter (named for the state where it is mined), and metalwork, including *kris* (knives or daggers with wavy blades and pistol handles).

Traditionally, Malaysian Chinese arts have been derived from Chinese civilizations. Recently, however, some Malaysian artists of Malay, Chinese, and Indian origin have begun to create new art forms that are syntheses of diverse cultures.

Traditional Malay dances have long been accompanied by music. For centuries, Malays have had orchestras that include drums, gongs, chimes, string instruments, oboes, flutes, and xylophones.

Perhaps the most renowned Peninsular Malaysian literary work is *Sejarah Melayu* ("Malay Annals"), written about 1535. The Annals present a detailed account of the beginnings of the city of Malacca. There is no written history or literature stemming from Sarawak and Sabah native cultures.

In addition to numerous Western literary works set in Malaysia, the Malays have produced considerable modern fiction and poetry.

Communication: Malaysia maintains a government-owned radio station, Radio Malaysia, and three television stations (one privately operated). All broadcast programs in many different languages.

Shortwave radio reception of Voice of America, BBC, AFRTS (American Forces Radio and Television Service), Radio Singapore, and Radio Australia are available.

There are 42 privately owned daily newspapers that vary greatly in circulation, news coverage, and quality. Laws forbidding the publishing of material considered harmful to Malaysia's morality, security, or order provide some restrictions for the press.

Transportation: As of 1990 Malaysia had 29,205 mi. (47,000 km) of roads, 80 percent of which are paved. The road network in Peninsular Malaysia is considered the best in Southeast Asia. Highways run from Kuala Lumpur to Seremban, from Kuala Lumpur to Karak, and from Jerangau to Jabor. Roads in Sarawak and Sabah tend to be of poor quality.

There are 1,666 mi. (2,681 km) of railway. On the mainland, Malaysian railways link Peninsular Malaysia with Singapore and Bangkok. Sarawak has no railway and Sabah has only a short line that connects Kota Kinabalu to Tenom.

Kuala Lumpur, George Town, and Kota Kinabalu have international airports.

There are several major coastal and river ports: George Town, Port Kelang, Port Dickson, and Malacca in Peninsular Malaysia; and Sandakan, Labuan, Kota Kinabalu, Tawau, Sibu, and Kuching in Sarawak and Sabah.

In rural areas, particularly in Sarawak and Sabah, water transport, the traditional means of Malaysian transportation, prevails. Many interior settlements are accessible only by river transport.

Schools: All public education is free and compulsory for children aged six to fifteen. As of 1980, about 44 percent of the population had received at least a primary education. Some children continue on to secondary school.

Higher education is offered by 25 teacher and technical colleges and by seven universities, the largest of which is the University of Malaya in Kuala Lumpur.

The Malay language is a compulsory subject in all school curricula. Religious education is compulsory for Muslim students.

As of 1980, Malaysia had a literacy rate of 75 percent for persons over age ten.

The literacy rate among males (83 percent) was higher than that among females (67 percent).

Health and Welfare: Most modern health services are provided by the government. In recent years the health of Malaysia has improved, with many diseases typical of tropical countries now eradicated. Yet diseases transmitted by insects or animals, such as malaria, still persist, particularly in rural areas.

Health conditions tend to be better in Peninsular Malaysia than in Sarawak and Sabah.

In 1981, major causes of death included heart disease, infectious and parasitic diseases, cancer, cerebrovascular diseases, and pneumonia.

ECONOMY AND INDUSTRY

Principal Products:

Agriculture: rubber, rice, cacao seeds, coconuts, palm oil, pepper, pineapples, timber
Manufacturing: cement, chemicals, textiles, rubber goods, processed foods
Mining: tin, petroleum, bauxite, copper, gold, iron

IMPORTANT DATES

4000 B.C. — First migrants move into area from southern China

2500 B.C. — Indian explorers reach Malaya

2000 B.C. — Migration of Malay ancestors from South China Sea islands

A.D. 800s — City-states develop along east and west coasts of the peninsula

1400-1500 — Malacca rises as a political power and commercial trading center. Islam is introduced along trade routes by missionaries and merchants

1400 — Parameswara establishes himself as ruler of Malacca

1446-1459 — Muzaffar Shah, Parameswara's great-grandson, rules Malacca

1509 — Portuguese set up a trading post in Malacca

1511 — Portuguese, led by Alfonso de Albuquerque, capture Malacca

1596 — Dutch secure a base on Java

1641 — Portuguese surrender Malacca to the Dutch who rule for 150 years

Late 1600s — Minangkabau from Sumatra migrate to Malaya

1700s — The Bugis from the Celebes Islands invade Malaya and establish the city-states of Selangor and Johore

1700s — Struggles among the Dutch, Bugis, Malays, and other tribes from Sumatra result in complete political fragmentation of the area

1786—Francis Light is the first Englishman to land on Pinang Island

1795—British capture Malacca

1819—British establish settlement in Singapore

1826—British form a colony that includes Malacca, Singapore, and Pinang Island

1800s-early 1900s—British gain control of nine peninsular Malay states as well as the area that is now Sarawak and Sabah

1800s—Opening of tin mines brings influx of Chinese miners to Malaya

1839—James Brooke, a British adventurer, lands in Sarawak

1840—Brooke named raja of Sarawak; begins 100 years of rule by Brooke family

1869—Opening of the Suez Canal

Late 1800s-early 1900s—Rubber plantations are developed in Malaya

1880-1920—Thousands of Indians migrate to work on rubber plantations

1896—Kuala Lumpur becomes capital of the Federated Malay States

December 7, 1941—Japanese attack Pearl Harbor and then invade Malaya

1945—Japanese surrender

1946—Creation of United Malaya National Organization (UMNO)

1948—Federation of Malaya proclaimed; consists of nine Malay states, Pinang, and Malacca

1948—Malayan Communist party begins terrorist campaign, known in Malaysia as "the Emergency," which lasts until 1960

1955—UMNO/MCA (Malayan Chinese Association) alliance carries national election against Malaya Communist party

August 31, 1957—Malaya is granted independence from Great Britain

1957—The "Malaya" name is modified to "Malaysia" when Sarawak and Sabah become part of the country

September 16, 1963—Malaysia is proclaimed an independent state consisting of the Federation of Malaya, Singapore, and the Sarawak and Sabah colonies

1963—Sukarno leads Indonesia against Malaysia

1965—Singapore withdraws from federation, becomes independent on August 9; Sukarno is overthrown

1971—Five-power (Malaysia, Singapore, New Zealand, Australia, and Great Britain) agreement developed to ensure Malaysia's defense against external aggression.

1989—Elected by hereditary rulers, Sulton Azlan Shah of Perak state becomes the ninth king of Malaysia on April 26, succeeding Mahmood Iskandar Ibni Sultan Ismail of Johor

1990—Elections result in a third term in office for Prime Minister

1992—Malaysia rebuffs a Netherlands proposal to regulate the harvesting of some of the nation's tropical timber; Parliament approves an amendment to the constitution to take effect at next elections that will increase the number of seats in the lower house from 180 to 192

1993—In partnership with Australia, Malaysia is to develop one of the largest undeveloped oil fields in Vietnam

1994—The nine hereditary sultans choose Sultan Jaafar bin Abdul Rahman as the tenth king of Malaysia; Malaysian Mining Corporation, a major producer of tin, announces that it will discontinue tin mining due to low global market prices; legislation is passed to permit armed forces more freedom in pursuing illegal loggers who smuggle hardwoods; contracts worth $1.5 billion are signed for British business in Malaysia

IMPORTANT PEOPLE

Alfonso de Albuquerque (1453-1515), led Portuguese invasion of Malacca in 1511

James Brooke (d.1868), British adventurer who became raja (leader) of Sarawak in 1840

Data Onn bin Jaafar, led Malay upsurge of political sentiment that culminated in the creation in 1946 of the United Malaya National Organization (UMNO)

Francis Light (c. 1740-1794), British adventurer who landed in Pinang in 1786 and developed that city and George Town as ports

Tan Cheng Lock, led Malayan Chinese Association (MCA) in an alliance with UMNO against the Malay Communist party in 1955

Muzaffar Shah (1445-?1459), ruled Malacca from 1446 to 1459

Tun Perak (d.1498), expanded Malacca control throughout Malay peninsula to island of Sumatra; maintained leadership role, 1456-98

Parameswara (d. 1424), began city of Malacca in 1403

Sir Thomas Stamford Raffles (1781-1826), an Englishman who established a settlement on Singapore Island in 1819

Tunku Abdul Rahman, led UMNO/MCA alliance in 1955 national election against Malaya Communist party; instrumental in developing Malaysia's superior school system

Raja Haji (d. 1784), Buginese leader who led Buginese invasions of Malay peninsula in 1700s

Achmed Sukarno (1901-70), president of Indonesia, 1945-65, and leader of Indonesian Communist party; led Indonesia against Malaysia in 1963; overthrown in 1965

Frederick Weld (1823-91), expanded British intervention throughout Malay peninsula

INDEX

Page numbers that appear in boldface type indicate illustrations

About the Author

David Wright was born on January 10, 1943, in Richmond, Indiana. He grew up in and around Richmond, graduating from high school in 1961. After he was graduated from Wittenberg University, Springfield, Ohio, in 1966, he was drafted and served two years in the United States army; one of the two years was spend in Vietnam. Wright has spent more than ten years in newspapers as a reporter, copy editor, and editor. Newspapers range from *The Chicago Tribune* to *The Monroe* (Wisconsin) *Times*. He has written one book for adults, *The Harley-Davidson Motor Company*, and has edited three children's books. He has about one hundred magazine articles to his credit on subjects ranging from vending machines to travel by motorcycle. He and his wife and two children live in West Bend, Wisconsin, an hour northwest of Milwaukee. Wright has been to Malaysia three times; he first visited the country while on "R & R" leave from Vietnam in 1967. His hobbies include hiking, traveling, fishing, reading, and writing. He has been a full-time free-lance writer, editor, and photographer for nine years.